SHONA GATES

HELLO ABUNDANCE

Simple rituals to BE more confident with money and wealth.

HELLO ABUNDANCE

CONTENTS

Foreword
ix
Dedication
x

1 — What if ?
1

2 — Once upon a time ...
2

3 — The Energy and Frequency of money
9

4 — Money Habits to call in Daily Abundance
14

5 — The 12 universal laws
27

6 — Self-Care – the foundation of everything.
36

7 — Energy cleansing
45

8 — Meditation + Manifestation
53

CONTENTS

9 — Decluttering – Releasing to receive
63

10 — Visualisation
74

11 — The Power of Affirmations and Positive Thoughts
85

12 — Angel Numbers + signs from the universe
99

13 — Raising Your Wealth Frequency
105

14 — Aligned pricing
112

15 — Selling with alignment
117

16 — Budgeting Like a Badass!
125

17 — How I manifested my dream home.
132

18 — What next ?
143

About The Author
147
Text Insert
148
NOTES
151
chapter
153

Copyright © 2021 by Shona Gates

All rights reserved. No part of this book may be reproduced in any manner whatsoever without written permission except in the case of brief quotations embodied in critical articles and reviews.
The information in this book was correct at the time of publication, but the author does not assume any liability for loss or damage caused by errors or omissions.

First Printing, 2021 www.sexyselfish.com

FOREWORD

As a busy business owner and mum, I know how the challenges in trying to remain positive in an increasingly complex world. I have worked with Shona Gates for 5 years on manifesting wealth and abundance. Through her mindfulness exercises, journalling, vision board workshops, training and courses, I have successfully learnt how to manifest money in my sleep (literally!) and create my dream business. My vision boards and thoughts are repeatedly coming true, and I don't know how it works exactly, and I don't need to know this, I just know that her teaching gets results.

Her methods and words of wisdom, (there is a reason I call her "the Oracle") work, if you take inspired action. I can confidently say reading this book will change your life and increase your abundance, without any woo-woo.

Amber Rushton - Award-Winning Entrepreneur

Dedicate to my girls

Lydia, Amber, Sandra, Jess & Sian

My soundboards, my cheerleaders, my soul tribe

And to my ever-supportive team

Danielle & Katrina

Thankyou x

WHAT IF ?

What if it just got to be easy?

What if the struggle just disappeared?

What if I got to wake up every day, and know that I'm enough, know that I have enough, and know that it was all going to be OK?

What if?

That's what you really have to ask yourself, are you brave enough to answer with honesty?

CHAPTER 2

ONCE UPON A TIME ...

Once upon a time, not so long ago really .... we were in the minus figures each week.

Hubby would get paid on Friday and by Tuesday there would be minus -$24.00, -$75.40, -$3.25

And then a big sigh of relief on Friday ...

And the cycle would begin again.

Now it's not as if we were sinking hundreds of dollars into the pokies, going out to dinner every night, shopping for clothes or buying fancy wine with all our money .... we were literally just paying bills, making it through, surviving ...

But we were definitely not living ...

So how did we go from minus figures every week, maxed

out credit card, etc. to the place we are in now where all of our bank accounts are growing?

We stood up for ourselves

We took responsibility for our situation

We didn't ask for a discount, or a special treatment

We didn't cry and feel sorry for ourselves

We didn't pull the "broke card"

Instead, we vowed to learn more about money, about budgets, and about bringing in more money.

We decided to learn all we could about the difference between people like us, who were barely scraping by, and people who were purchasing their third investment property …

I researched, learned, and experimented with the "energy of abundance" and how it differed from the mindset and actions of scarcity.

It started with what we could access for free, library books, free webinars, podcasts, YouTube. Then we invested all the spare money we had, in buying books about finance, about investing, money mindset, and business. I also took online courses paid to work with mentors.

Some weeks we chose to spend the money we were using to pay off debt, to instead invest in me and working with a mentor or buying an online program to help me gain more knowledge to help us.

We decided to break the cycle.

Break the cycle of poor me

Break the cycle of lack

Break the cycle of hand outs

Break the cycle of "why does this happen to us"

Did we do it for us? Yes, but mostly we did it for our kids.

We wanted to show them what can happen when you take responsibility and become empowered around something that made you feel powerless.

To show them that you can learn about anything and acquire any skill you really desire.

To teach them that the world doesn't owe them anything, I mean just existing here is a privilege, it's not a right.

We wanted to make it absolutely crystal clear that if you want something to change in this world, like really truly change ... it comes down to YOU.

Your decisions

Your habits

Your actions

No one else can make that change for YOU ...

And I admit,

We aren't out of the woods yet; we have a long way to go before we are holidaying in bora bora and hitting that 3rd investment property. But instead of buying a lotto ticket and hoping it might happen, Now I know it WILL happen, without a doubt. Because not only are we manifesting it ... but we are taking the inspired action to actually achieve it.

Are you?

Are you ready to step fully into the reality of being a wealthy woman?

are you really truly ready to attract more abundance into your life?

Yes of course you are because you wouldn't be reading this book if you weren't.

There are plenty of people with great jobs that can't seem to have, keep, or save money.

There are a lot of people with large incomes that worry about money day in and day out.

There are plenty of responsible smart people who follow a budget but can't seem to pay off debt past a certain point or grow savings beyond a certain point.

It can happen to any of us.

That's because money isn't just about numbers, strategy, and restriction. Money is about energy, frequency, and embodiment.

What I am here to teach you, will revolutionize your entire life, and not just your money mindset.

I know what it's like to feel financially suffocated in your career or business. To dread looking at your bank accounts, and to experience guilt and fear around spending money whether it was for something you needed or something you wanted. While I've been applying manifestation principles to creating what I want for my entire life (I totally vision boarded my husband) **applying these new realities with money, was a whole new ball game for me.**

It challenged everything I thought I knew about myself, and about how I thought the world worked.

I had self-doubt.

I had self-worth issues.

I had an identity around being a "stay at home mum" who wasn't worthy of abundance.

But despite all of that, and maybe truthfully because all of that,

I have dedicated myself to putting the work towards having an empowered money mindset.

It's time to heal your history with money, understand the frequency and vibration of money, rework your mindset around money, and set into reality a new blueprint for how you spend, save, earn, receive, release, relate and manifest money in your life. ?

I love this work. I love it in a way I cannot even begin to explain to you.

It's truly one of the reasons I feel I am alive. And I am thankful beyond measure to use it to help you transform this area of your life.

Because the truth is, this isn't really about money.

It's about freedom, opportunity, and choice.

It's about not having to say "no" to the desires of your heart any longer.

Money is a resource to me. Money is my friend and ally.

Money helps me pay people, design my life, support others, and get my work out into this world in a BIG way. Money amplifies the best part of me, my kind heart, my empathy, my responsibility, all of them become GREATER with money. What strengths will be amplified for you?

My relationship with money has become a joyful expression of creating, expecting, receiving, and giving.?Today, it is one of the most rewarding, fun, and reliable parts of my life.?And now I want to help it become that way for you too.

So, let's GO ALL IN.

We are meant to.

And we're worthy.

No holding back.

The time is now.

CHAPTER 3

THE ENERGY AND FREQUENCY OF MONEY

The frequency of money

The energy of abundance

Buzz words and marketing phrases thrown around everywhere in the online spiritual entrepreneur and manifestation space.

But you see the thing is, those two terms mean totally different things.

And while no one else wants to talk about it, I'm going to. Because to shift your energy and rewire your abundance frequency, you first have to understand, clearly and completely, what they actually are.

So, I'm going to try and wrap up a decade of personal development research and my own experimentation into 2 definitions.

Energy

Energy consists of the conscious choices and actions to feel good and to shift our "energy" from low to high, from sadness to hopefulness, from despair to gratitude, and from negative to positive.

Things like making a gratitude list, listening to music that puts you in a good mood, meditating, having sex, going for a walk-in nature, watching a funny movie, having a hot bubble bath, saying affirmations, and creating a vision board. All of this is the Energy, working to help us tap into the feelings of abundance.

Frequency

Frequency is the subconscious vibration that we put out into the universe and it either attracts or repels abundance every day. We are essentially a gigantic radio tower. Every moment of every day we are sending out a signal via our subconscious thoughts, actions, and belief systems. The signal can be changed, but it takes the emotional work to first identify those limiting money beliefs, trace the origin, call them out and then rewrite new ones.

If you're reading this book because you were first a fan of my previous work "Goodbye Money Guilt" you'll know what I'm talking about. * Insert shameless book plug

Because that book dives deep into the "frequency" work of releasing money shame, transforming your relationship with wealth and creating a positive abundance mindset.

5 years ago, when I was drafting my first money mindset book, it slipped out of the "personal development section" and was heading more towards fantasy novel trilogy set. It was too big, too burly, too scary, and too intimidating, so I broke it down. And while it was tempting to release "Hello abundance" first, due to its easy marketability and fun concepts,

I decided not to, because while the energy work is fun, and feels good ... often the frequency work, is not.

It is harder, there are often tears, it's diving into your past, asking yourself to answer questions with a radical honesty that most of us never want to face. The frequency work is less sellable, it's harder to swallow, and more difficult to share... but like the stubborn and tenacious person that I am, of course I chose that one first.

Because the energy work does great things, but the energy work on top of a solid foundation of subconscious frequency work ... well that will move mountains, rattle the stars, and shift you into a state of abundance on every level that you never knew was possible.

This book is a lot more fun, and has less profound paradigm shifts, and more aha feel good moments.

Unlike my first book "Goodbye Money Guilt" which was a transformational process, chapter by chapter, that focused on identifying and healing your subconscious limiting beliefs around money, and worthiness, this book – "Hello Abundance" is more of a weekend read, open to any chapter, skip to the section you like style book.

We are going to cover a lot, from goal setting to angel numbers, and decluttering for manifestation to creating your first vision board.

This book is the "how" to "Goodbye Money Guilts" ... "Why"

The energy to the frequency.

The action plan to the inner soul searching.

These teachings have been the focus of my Sexy Selfish Elite membership, an online community for mums and women in business, who are interested in alignment and abundance. Each month we focus on one core topic and dedicate the entire month to learning about it, implementing it, and sharing it with each other.

In the Elite membership we have both mums, and mums in business, so you may notice some of the chapters have language around business, aligned selling, confidence in marketing, etc. while the language may or may not be different than what you might be used to, the principals and the energy is universal. So, I'm excited to take these tried and tested techniques, focuses and guides, to help you on your journey to not only transform your relationship with money, but say hello to Abundance on every single level.

Read it cover to cover,

Dedicate a month or a week to each chapter,

Or simply open when you need a bit of inspiration. Chances are you'll land in the exact chapter you need.

It doesn't matter how you use it,

there is magic in these pages, and in the in-between.

Shall we begin ...

CHAPTER 4

MONEY HABITS TO CALL IN DAILY ABUNDANCE

So many beautiful clients of mine are doing all the right things, charging their crystals, saying their affirmations, journaling and tapping into their inner wealthy woman. But, when I ask them what their financial goal is for the year, or how much money they have invested, or even if they know how many of X product have been sold ... they look at me like a deer caught in the headlights.

There seems to be this idea that if you're just spiritual enough, or just focus on the abundance and feelings of wealth enough ... you can ignore the actual money side, but still somehow end up mega rich. As if wishing on a star was enough to hit those 6 figures.

We treat it as if it's an either-or situation.

Either you focus on your money, track every penny and it becomes obsessive, or you do the spiritual work, ignore your money, say no to budgets and the wealth will manifest.

What a lie!

What a lie!

What a lie!

It's really more of a spectrum. And like most spectrums, each end of it can be pretty severe and probably detrimental to actually achieving your desires. However, we can cultivate this delicious middle zone where we create healthy money habits that help us track our progress and stay spiritually aligned in a more balanced place of gratitude and excitement.

First let's identify your current money habits ....

Answer these questions or think about them for some revealing insights into your relationship with money. Yes babe, you're in a relationship with money whether you realise it or not.

Do you check your bank account regularly? 10 times a day or maybe once a week?

Do you know what bills you have to pay, when they are due, how much is owed?

Do you know how much money you make on average each month?

Do you know how much you spend on expenses vs. luxe experiences?

When was the last time you thought about money?

How do you feel when you spend money?

How do you feel when you make money?

How do you feel when other people talk about money?

The answers to these can shed a lot of light on your current relationship status with money, and show if you are in a committed, respectful, balanced, nurturing, and supportive relationship with money ... or it is more along the lines of "its complicated", toxic, neglectful, includes mind games, ignoring and/or desperately clinging, full of frustration, anger, and resentment?

You are where you are right now, and that's OK.

This is not a place for shame, or judgment.

This is a place of learning differently so we can do things differently.

But let's just cut out the bullshit and mind games here and get really honest.

If money was your partner, would it love you or despise you?

If money was your BFF, would it dump you or invite you on a girls trip?

If money was trying to be in your life and yet you kept pushing it away ... how long do you think it would last before it just gave up?

Identifying our current relationship with money is one of the first steps to moving forward. Take a deep breath and acknowledge where you're currently at. Take a moment, sit with it, feel it out ... and then ask yourself,

Is this really serving me ....?

Am I ready for a paradigm shift?

It's time to step into the abundant woman, the higher self, the inner rich bitch that is calling out to you and start treating money like your BFF.

It's not about creating a ridged, obsessive, one size fits all, stage 5 clinger relationship, but instead one with balance, harmony, flexibility, support and mostly neutrality.

When I was a child, our boat nearly capsized and sank while fishing one day. It was terrifying, suddenly the safety and neutrality of 'the boat' that I had always known in my childhood, felt unbalanced. I felt too large for the boat, there were too many people, it was too wavy, ... and all these fears were there despite the fact that "I can swim" (rather well actually), but for years the panic around boats and water consumed me. I couldn't even be near boats let alone go in one, and yet despite not being able to set foot in one, I would use up an abnormal amount of energy and brainpower worrying about it.

Eventually, in my late teens I sought professional help, and with my supportive boyfriend by my side (now husband, who loved fishing, boating, and everything involving water) we made a plan ....

Exposure therapy.

We created 10 steps, that were a little like this ... be near the boat, be near the boat on the trailer, sit in the boat on the trailer, watch it going into the water, stand in the water near the boat (familiarise myself with sounds and feeling of waves), sit in the boat in the shallows, moored (not going) allow myself a few hours like this, hear the boat going, get in the boat with minimal people, going slow, then going faster, then more turns.

It took time, but I got there.

Keep in mind that this happened over a period of about 5-6 years. It did not happen overnight, there were many panic attacks, tears, anxiety moments, full body shaking, flashbacks, and sneaky moments of joy and pride scattered throughout there. It's a gradual process, but my fear of boats has been greatly diminished. Heck, sometimes even for a few moments I actually enjoy myself out on the water.

The point was to get over my fear and move past it. I had to expose myself to it time and time again in a controlled way to gain the strength and confidence to dissipate that fear. I had to do the same thing 5 years ago with my money ... I was in this toxic cycle of obsessively checking my accounts (you'll do that when you have 0 money in them and every cent counts). I needed to expose myself to money in a way that was a little more structured, controlled, and gentle than the binge or ignore cycle I had been following.

"Every day at 8 am, morning coffee, check the accounts ... no excuses,

It will take less than 5 minutes, I'll be grateful for everything I have, even if it isn't much, because the more grateful I am, the more money I can attract to me"

I set the alarm, and every day at 8, I logged into the app and checked my bank. Some days there would be $400, other days $40, and some days $4.

But every day I repeated the same sentence to myself.

"I am so grateful for all the money I have in my life, all the opportunities, experiences, and choices I get to have because of it. I love money and money loves me"

5 years later, every day when I have my morning coffee my fingers automatically open my online banking on my phone. It's a ritual now, that started off as a habit.

I've seen my bank account with $2.75 in it, I've also seen it with $155,000 in it ... and guess what, thanks to this exposure type therapy and all the work I've done on my money mindset, opening that account on those two different days felt exactly the same.

"I am so grateful for all the money I have in my life, all the opportunities, experiences, and choices I get to have because of it. I love money and money loves me"

After doing this for several years, I've noticed I no longer panic when my bank accounts get low. The benefit of doing this every day for so long is that you notice the patterns, you see the bigger picture ... sometimes the accounts are low, sometimes they are high, some days, weeks, months, you don't spend a lot of money, other days, weeks, months you do.

There are peaks and troughs, winters and summers, like all patterns in life...

It doesn't mean anything about me as a person.

It doesn't affect me morally or my worthiness.

It neutralised my emotional response to the ebb and flow of money.

Another part of this cycle was learning to track my money.

Not in an obsessive, budgeting, counting every penny, cutting back every cent you can, cash envelope scarcity way ... but tracking my money to be able to "see" and "collect evidence" of the abundance coming into my life.

I challenged myself to pay attention to my money in just an observant neutral way, not getting attached, not getting emotional and just holding on loosely. I had this excel spread sheet and I put it up on my fridge. Each day I logged into my business accounts and personal accounts to track any money that had come in.

It was a big eye opener for me, especially realising just how many different ways money came into our accounts each month.

We had my husband's wage,

My husband's business income,

Centrelink payments,

Residual cheques from my past MLM work,

Book royalties from "goodbye money guilt",

Commissions from blog pieces I had done for websites like MAMAMIA,

And then my sexy selfish income too.

6 months ago, I added another facet to my business with the design work I do, and we are now working on another stream of income to add in as I write this.

On top of that, there were even random cheques from things I had forgotten about, like an old bond payment, and then a bonus I wasn't expecting.

That's when the belief that "money flows into my life every day from expected and unexpected ways" really solidified for me and became my truth.

I had the evidence

I knew it was true

And it was my reality

Money tracking feels like something that can very easily slip into the negative, obsessive, or toxic. But if you hold the perspective and remember to emotionally detach and see if you can kind of view it as an experiment or research instead ... it can be SUPER POWERFUL.

Give it a go, I'm excited to see what happens for you.

MY DAILY MONEY RITUALS

- Wake up, don't press snooze, immediately say *"thank you"*, gratitude first thing in the morning instantly puts me in a higher vibration, and make coffee. As I stir my coffee, I draw a star with my spoon and whisper abundance affirmations into it, like a little magic intention fused spell *"you are a badass, today is going to be amazing, the more fun you have the more money you will make"*.

- As I drink my coffee, I check my two bank accounts and my business sales for the day, expressing gratitude for all that I have not and all that is on its way to me.

- And then there is mum life stuff ... Including listening to my favourite playlist on the drive to school.

- Once Hudson goes down for his nap, I take 20 minutes to drink coffee number two, listen to high vibe abundance frequencies on Spotify, and journal, brain dump, tap in, script, etc. The soul work before the strategy has been one of the most powerful shifts for me.

- Movement breaks through the day, earthing my

feet on the bare ground, stretching, some yoga poses, a workout, sex, or just dancing around with my baby. Circulating that energy and making sure I'm not getting stagnant.

- Lunch without any work. So, either while reading a book, or watching some mindless reality TV. Something to tune in and rest.

- Work with intention. I set regular timers on my phone to make sure I'm working, then breaking, working, then breaking and not getting burnt out. 20-minute intervals are the magic number for me, but yours might be different.

- At dinner time we go around the table and take turns asking each other what the best parts of our day was, this is a great practice to encourage gratitude in your family.

- After dinner when I've cleaned up the kitchen, and organised my coffee for the morning, that's when I complete my money tracking. So, I once again log into my accounts and business systems to see how the day progressed. I brain dump anything "to manifest" that needs to get forwarded to my assistant and sketch out my outcomes for the next day.

- When my day is ending, I like to take a nice hot cleansing shower. I visualise the day and any worries washing off my skin, and then before I hop out the shower, I use that space and intention to create my new reality (quantum leaping in the shower is totally a thing), I see my vision board (that is on my shower glass) and affirm money mantras to myself before taking deep breaths and hopping out to my new reality.

These little pockets of my day mean so much to me. They have helped me shift my entire reality from broke and fearful for the future, to abundance, hopeful and grateful every day.

We are told that one special course, program, retreat weekend, coach, mentor, etc. will gift us the transformation we desire. But it's not something that can be gifted to us, and it's not something that happens fast. It happens slowly, a build-up of momentum, turning activities into rituals which then become habits and rewire our subconscious beliefs. It's a day by day, moment by moment choice.

It happened for me because every day I woke up and I chose to run my day instead of my day running me.

You have that choice too, so make it count.

-

CHAPTER 5

THE 12 UNIVERSAL LAWS

Have you seen that movie with Brendan Fraser and Alicia Silverstone, "blast from the past"?

In the movie this younger boy has been living in a bunker for 30 years, growing up with only his mum and dad, rations and 4 walls underground. He believes the world they used to know was destroyed, so when construction workers dig up the bunker and he's pulled out, he quickly learns that the world is a lot bigger than he ever thought possible.

That's what we are going to do here today, we are blasting the bunker right open.

And what you're about to see and learn, you will not be able to unlearn again.

We all know gravity, it works, it's all around us every day, we trust it, it works whether we believe in it or not.

These 12 universal laws are the same.

Everyone and their aunt have watched the secret, has heard of, or know about the law of attraction, but that's just 1 of these 12 laws ... so I'm going to share them with you today.

The secret tells us that visualisation will give us what we want, just wish for it and it will come true. So, we wish ... and it doesn't come true, so we throw our hands up in the air and call bullshit on it all.

The first time I heard about the secret I think I laugh snorted into my G+T and called it a bunch of "new age bullshit" ... It took me a few more years before I revisited the concept with an open heart and began to see it for what it really is.

An opportunity to consciously create your reality.

Being a powerful manifestor, is about a combination of choosing your desires, and then taking inspired action, not picking and choosing the laws as if choosing from a fast-food menu but embracing all of them. Because whether we want to acknowledge them or not, they are all working, every moment of every day, with or without our conscious validation.

Curious? want to learn more about these mysterious forces running our reality?

Here's my cheat sheet. (Just keep in mind that it is an overview and if we were to deep dive into this, it would be a book by itself).

THE 12 UNIVERSAL LAWS

The law of oneness – we are all connected, we are all the same, we all have the power within us to create magic, so it also means that what you do to others you do to yourself. If you're gossiping or hurting others, you may as well be doing it to yourself. Celebrate people creating wealth or manifesting what you desire because that means you can achieve it too.

The law of vibration – everything is vibrating, we just can't see the vibration of the atoms. But those vibrations radiate out 24/7. There is no such thing as stillness in our universe, even the universe itself is constantly in motion, constantly expanding. We are just one big ball of energy. To magnetise what you desire you need to align your vibration with the vibration of what you want to attract. You do that by feeling really freaking good about what you desire. When you are an energetic match, you activate the law of attraction. Trust the vibes, you have felt it before when you met someone and got a bad vibe, or you met someone and felt really safe, this is it.

The law of action – so many spiritual teachers ignore this. When we ignore it, we create resistance. The universe desires some physical inspired movement to shift energy and create momentum. Not all "action" is equal, Inspired ACTION is more important than just fast ACTION. You must listen to those soul nudges. Inspired action can be many different things, like creating a resume, mentioning to a friend you're looking for a new apartment in X area, trusting an impulse to meet a friend for coffee that ends up with you bumping into an old school friend who then wants to hire you. Trust those nudges, take inspired action, move forward, and have faith that the universe is fully supporting and co-conspiring to deliver what you desire.

The law of correspondence – this law states that your outer world will only ever reflect your inner world. You need to change the internal first. You can't force it physically without shifting your perspective and energy around it. Practising forgiveness (yeah, I know, eyeroll, another spiritual babe talking about forgiveness, but there's a reason this topic is so popular). Forgiveness gives you space in your life to accept abundance in… what happens in your mind will be reflected in your reality. Keep tabs on your energy and realign when you need to, whether it's with music movement, journaling all of it, etc. to shift your energy. Remember that It's all connected.

The law of cause and effect – karma, you reap what you sow. The soil doesn't care, it doesn't have a preference, it will grow what is planted. If you plant positivity, you will grow positivity, if you plant resentment, bitchiness, and fear you will grow more of that. Focus on the harvest that you want, not the one you **don't** want.

The law of attraction – like attracts like, the universe doesn't have bias, what you send out it will send back. If your reality is filled with things you don't want, it doesn't mean anything bad about you or what you will attract, don't let it mean anything, just check your energy, and realign with what you desire to call in. Be ok with where you are, while you call in the next level of you. One of my biggest breakthrough moments in my first book "Goodbye Money Guilt" was when I shared about my toxic, needy, clingy, and obsessive relationship with money. I realised that if I treated someone I cared about, the same way I was treating money, they would probably run in the opposite direction. I had to shift my mindset and how I related to money before more could come into my life. Once I did this, the whole game changed.

The law of perpetual transmutation – nothing is static, everything is always changing, to live is to change. We are constantly in transition, you know we all have that one person in our life that is just waiting for next month, waiting until they move, waiting until after Christmas, waiting until after the holiday, waiting until things settle down .... But life never truly settles down. This law puts the power back in our hands. We can change things the moment we decide to change them. We can transmute negative energy into positive immediately. And high vibe energy will always transmute low vibes. The fear and perception that low vibes bring you down is a false reality you have subscribed to ... not truth. Keep focusing on your own energy and like a shining light house, you will guide and can inspire others too. Everything in our world today began in someone's imagination and mind first ... remember that.

The law of compensation, similar to cause and effect – monetary rewards, compensation gifts, etc. Give what you want to receive freely. Too many expectations and perceived lack of gratitude block our blessings. This law also reminds us that our work is divinely guided. It is a high service, and we do deserve to be compensated for that. We do not owe people affordability, and we do not need to validate and justify our pricing beyond making sure it is truly aligned with our heart.

The law of relativity - states that every single soul on this planet will face is challenging from time to time, but it's all relative, nothing is as bad as it seems. We are always in transitions, everyone faces challenges, obstacles, and problems, see them with a different perspective. They help us grow and up-level our skills, they are a bump on the road. Challenges can suck, yes, those feelings are valid, but remember that it is making you grow, this is the level up. You grow through what you go through. And just because someone may have it "worse" than you do, it doesn't discount that what you are feeling and experiencing is very real. What is bad for you, might be great circumstances for someone else and vice versa.

The law of polarity — every single thing in this universe has its polar opposite, joy has sadness, up has down, light has dark. Many people get frustrated that polar opposites exist, but the universe does this to serve us. We will get what we don't want in order to have crystal clarity on what we do want, and so we can have gratitude for it when we experience it. Those spring days feel extra warm and glorious because of the winter months.

The law of rhythm — everything has cycles, nature has cycles, and we are nature. You are NOT going to feel high vibe, kicking ass and taking names every single day. Some days you are going to be super inspired and feel like FIRE, some days you are going to be inspired to rest. We don't have 365 days of summer, flowers don't bloom every day, we also need winter to be able to harvest. The bad days don't last forever and neither do the good days, but that's ok … see it for what it is, you cannot force motivation sometimes. Sometimes you are being called to step back and rest. This is ok!

The law of gender — everything has both masc and fem energy, macs/action, and fem/allowing co-existence. Our job is to find the balance, dance between both patience and persistence. Embodying one or the other will leave us either stagnant or pushing too hard to the point that we are exhausted. It is equal parts inspired action and receiving and allowing.

As I look back over my life, I can clearly see all the moments dotted along my journey where these laws were in effect. Little reminders that the universe does have my back, to be kind to others, to take power over my journey and my future, to express gratitude for what I have while working towards what I want, to take aligned inspired action, and allow myself to be at peace with the slow, restful hibernation periods in life, knowing that the energy, flow, and adventure will shine again soon.

Believe it or not, the universe is actually working in your favour. It doesn't want you to suffer in fear, it wants you to be abundant, successful, happy, and living your best life.

It's time to have a little more trust.

In the universe

In your divine power

And in your own intuition and self

You've got this!

SELF-CARE – THE FOUNDATION OF EVERYTHING.

We've come a long way don't get me wrong, but as modern women, we are still on the back foot. We are so desensitized to our needs that often; our boundaries don't exist. We put the kids, work, husband, and the dog first until we realize it's been 3 hours since we needed to go the toilet and it has been eight months since we got a full night's sleep.

But no more.

To be the best mum, woman, business owner and abundant badass we can be, we need ourselves in TIP TOP condition. How do we achieve that...? self-care.

REMEMBER THIS: Your energy is essential.

Self-love/care isn't all about thinking you're the sexiest thing to walk this planet, nor is it about trying to be. It's about acknowledging who you are ... the exact version of you. And allowing yourself to be entirely whoever that is! It's seeing your weaknesses as room for improvement & loving yourself enough to build upon them! It's turning the perspective you have of your 'flaws' into an appreciation for quirky treasures of your unique self!

Love is unconditional, so self-love takes forgiveness.

It takes accepting that what's done is done & loving yourself enough to move past the mistakes you've made and focus on new beginnings. Self-love brings pride, not arrogance, not false confidence, and not boastfulness... A proud you is an uncapped you, an uncensored beauty, powerful energy, a magnetic being, an irreplaceable, jaw-dropping, show-stopping, non-replicable, fricken amazing YOU!

So here is some real talk about how I fit self-love into my day.

Now keep in mind, I am a MUM, I have 3 kids, all of which have special needs. So, factor in 9 separate therapy appointments every fortnight plus ... school drop-offs, athletics, ballet class, cricket practice, playgroup AGM meetings, oh and I run 2 companies.

There are definitely times where my self-care has slid to the bottom of the list, ironically those were also the times my business felt stagnant, my relationship grew tense, and the flow of money seemed to turn into more of a trickle than a stream.

Self-care is important, maybe even more important than the right fakebook add strategy (yeah, I said that).

If I can fit in self-care every day, so can you.

EASIER SAID THAN DONE RIGHT!

Because self-love (when as women, we are so used to putting ourselves last), is HARD, Legit hard. Because for some reason (that I'm not going to go into today because it requires an entire lecture of its own), we have been hard wired to put our self last. To put kids, friends, family, housework, study, our partners and picking up those bloody dirty socks off the floor … again … first! I mean when was the last time you held off going to the toilet? Seriously, I can't be the only one who does this? you needed to go, you know you needed to go, but first you made that phone call, finished that report, put a load in the washing machine, and made the toddlers some snacks …. then it got to the point where you literally almost peed yourself and you had to run to the bathroom.

Don't worry, no judgment. We have all been there. Why do we put off everything until it's too late? … We delay, delay, delay … until we either pee ourselves or in the case of self-care, end up having a total breakdown.

No one else is going to do this for you, it's up to you to prioritise it.

What does this have to do with money and abundance ... EVERYTHING!

How we do anything is how we do everything ... repeating "I am a wealthy confident badass woman" in front of your mirror every day might be a good idea, but if you don't back it up with the micro decisions in your day, all you're going to be doing is confusing the shit out of the universe.

Abundant affirmation - *"Money flows to me every day"*.

Scarcity in reality - Is still wearing a holey maternity bra when your child is 8 and hasn't BF for 7 years.

Abundant affirmation *"I nourish my body and mind"*.

Scarcity in reality – is running yourself ragged, staying up till 10 pm cutting cucumber into dinosaur shapes for the kids' lunches, but skipping breakfast, and eating the toddlers' crusts for lunch because you forgot to feed yourself all day.

The messages don't add up. We need to walk our talk and start treating ourselves like the most abundant, badass versions of ourselves. It's time to stop delaying ... YOU are important ... and you deserve to be overflowing with self-love NOW .... and not just the busting to pee kind of overflowing.

Self-care can be a hard concept to grasp at the start. Despite the shelves in Kmart being lined with books about mindfulness, it's easier said than done. Even working though, the mental blocks of *"but I don't have time, but I don't have money, but I have kids who literally are stuck to me all day long"* can be exhausting and take time. And never fear, we will circle back to deal with those excuses soon. First, I want to assure you that whatever your excuses and resistance may be right now, self-care, self-love and YOU are more important than the bullish*t story you are telling yourself right now. But let's start slow ... let's ease you into it.

First, you need to realize that YOU are perfect, YOU are beautiful and yes you are worthy of love, success, health, wealth, and abundance. Picture your child, or if you don't have kids, your niece, nephew, or God child ... picture yourself as a small child, about 4-5 ... do you see how beautiful they are? do you see how perfect they are?

All the wonder in their eyes, how open they are to love and the kindness in the world. Now, picture their face or their crushed little soul every time you call them fat, ugly, worthless, disgusting, stupid, unloved.

How do you think this small child would react to such words???

How would your daughter, your niece, or your best friend feel if you treated them the way you treat yourself???

Wouldn't they be hurt and want to resist, shut down, or lash out in anger?

Your thoughts create your reality and when you are speaking to your body and yourself in a self-critical or dismissive manner, you are just being a bully to yourself ... and no one likes a bully, so it's time to stop being your own worst enemy.

When you speak to yourself and treat yourself the way you would love your child or someone you care for, your body loves you back, you smile more, you feel more attractive, open, connected ... suddenly you might even find your skin glowing and your body getting healthier. Your thoughts are important, so monitor them closely ... remember you are in control of them ... and you can choose to stop those negative patterns.

Exercise ...No, not that type of exercise, calm down, I'm not going to make you do hill sprints EWWW

Let's start with some easy exercises to get you started. Each day pick one and commit to it fully. If you have a partner, explain that you're trying something new that is important to you and you would appreciate their support with your exercises ... most of these only take 15-30 minutes ... so, plan ahead if you need to book that time with a sitter or your partner.

- **Pause + Sip** – Make a cup of tea or coffee and drink it sitting outside in nature with no distractions. Spend 5 minutes drinking and looking at the clouds.
- **Mask it Up** – Give yourself a face mask....there are plenty of DIY face masks on Pinterest that you can do using basic ingredients from around the home.
- **Walk it off** – Go for a walk. One of the best ways to get your endorphins flowing. Get your blood pumping + bonus points for fresh air and nature....crank the beats in your headphones or just enjoy the silence.
- **Hot + Soapy** – Take a nice hot shower, add some lavender oil, and wash away all the worry of the day, scrub, shave, moisturize and really pamper yourself.

So simple, but often with simple things, if it's easy to do it's just as easy not to do.

How did you feel?

Inspired?

Invigorated?

More awake?

More connected?

More energetic ....?

That's the power of self-care ... that is your body, mind, and spirit Saying "*THANK YOU, FINALLY, SHE GETS IT... TOOK THIS CHICK LONG ENOUGH* "Your body and soul are literally jumping for joy right now!!

Now all those exercises were pretty much FREE, it just cost you a bit of time ... and probably a negotiation with your partner about keeping the kids out of your bedroom for half an hour ... but at the end of the day you didn't have to outlay thousands of dollars or head away on a fortnight-long silent yoga retreat to start to feel better about yourself ... did you?

Self-care can be these big moments, like going on your first solo holiday, ordering meal prep for the first time, saying no, and setting healthy boundaries. But it can also be all these little moments in between. Using the drier even though the sun is out because you are time poor and exhausted, shutting off your lap top early and going to sleep before 11, turning away a client that you know will be more trouble than they are worth, etc.

Self care isn't just about you. Your kids, your work mates, your family, your friends, and your partner all feed off the energy that you put out ... when you are happy, they are happier too...

SELF LOVE IS SELFLESS!

Being selfish for a minimum of 30 minutes a day ... makes you more selfless for the other 23.5 hours. So, take those 30 minutes and make it for YOU. Whatever it is that lights you up, grounds you, and fills your cup.

Take it ...

You don't need my permission, you don't need anyone's permission, but here I'll give it to you just in case. You have full permission to take at least 30 minutes every day just for YOU. Without validation, justification, or guilt.

CHAPTER 7

ENERGY CLEANSING

The first time I ever heard of using sage as something other than a seasoning for holiday dishes, it was in my childhood, during a visit to my mother's friend "Aunty Linda". Aunty Linda was into all the cool witchy stuff (it was the 90s and every girl, including me, was obsessed with charmed). She was telling me about using sage to cleanse any clothes or items if I had bought them from a second-hand shop. She explained that we could use sage to cleanse away the previous owner's energy, and make sure the clothes and items were ready for our own energy with a clean slate.

My mum rolled her eyes, but to me it made complete sense.

My dad didn't agree with Aunty Linda's *"witchy stuff"*, but I always thought she was a badass. So understandably, I wasn't allowed to splurge my hard-earned Christmas money on *"devil summoning herbs"*. White sage bundles were not something you could easily get in a small-town in Australia in the 90s, a long way before eBay, Etsy, and amazon delivered things straight to your door. Therefore, I made do with some white sage oil I found in a store and created a spray bottle.

After any thrift store expeditions, or after receiving any black plastic bags full of hand-me-downs from my older cousins, I would religiously spray everything with my sage oil spray.

It makes me smile to think back to the secret baby witch version of me that hid crystals in her knickers draw and studied love spells. About 15 years later, I was scrolling Instagram stories on a full moon and came across a friend Erin who was walking around her home with a bundle of herbs, fanning smoke around the rooms of her house.

Something lit up inside me, something felt right, so I sent her a message *"what's the smoke all about"* I asked, and she told me, and I ordered some online about 5 minutes later....

Suddenly I was reconnected with the baby witch inside me,

Every new car, new home, new crystal, second-hand item, etc. gets a thorough sage cleansing when it arrives at my house, and each new/full moon, mummy does all her "smelly witchy stuff".

Sage cleansing is the spiritual equivalent of washing your hands or having a nice hot shower at the end of a busy, stressful, sweaty day. It's basically "Energy hygiene" and hell yes, it's important.

In a general life sense, a spiritual sense, and of course a money sense.

So, what is "sage cleansing"? where did it come from? and how do I do it?

Burning sage is one of the oldest, purest, and most consistent methods of cleansing a person, space, or group (even unwanted spirits). The practice dates to cavemen days and early humans. Sage has been used in many indigenous cultures in all corners of the world for thousands of years.

So yeah, it's nothing new. Sage clears bacteria in the air. Scientists have even proven that sage can clear up to 94% of airborne bacteria in the space. When white sage is burned, it releases negative ions. If you are a bit of a nerd like me, you'll know that it is linked to putting people in a more positive mood.

When it comes to buying something to cleanse your space with, there are lots of options, from making your own to using something from your own native culture...

However, the most well-known (and for a good reason) is white sage. No, not the sage from your kitchen, there is a particular type you want. Look for California white sage or white sage smudge stick, it can come in an actual bundle of leaves, an incense, twig, cone, or herb concoction. All these ways will work, so find one that suits you and your style.

I use a mix of white sage oil, Incense sticks and leaves, and smudge stick. While it can be super tempting to use BIG online stores like Amazon, Wish, or eBay to order your sage tools, I encourage you to avoid large commercial vendors. They aren't concerned with the quality or sacredness of these materials, and it is not a priority to them if they are ethically sourced.

Intention and energy matters, even when you are purchasing the items for your spiritual work.

A note on Palo Santo. You'll notice I don't recommend the use of Palo Santo. I previously used this a lot, and in fact, still have a few sticks leftover. However, a friend of mine brought my attention to the abuse and destruction of the sacred Palo Santo trees. After doing my research, I decided not to add to this problem by choosing to no longer buy or use Palo Santo in my spiritual work. If you desire to use Palo Santo, I recommend doing your research and making sure it has been ethically sourced.

Prep work... Now anyone who has worked with me before, knows I'm a bit of a rebel; I'm a total fuck the rules kind of girl. But then, there is also the inner witchy cycle part of me that also loves a Lil bit of routine.

So, I always take the "rules" more as guidelines. Many people will say you can only sage cleanse on particular days, like full moon, new moon, etc. For a lot of us starting, this is a simple system to follow ... however, sometimes you have a shitty day, sometimes you feel a little stagnant, flat, and blah, or sometimes you're dealing with some heavy emotional shit ... and that type of stuff needs to be dealt with asap. It doesn't matter "when" or really "how" you do this because there is no right or wrong. There's only intention and energy.

Sage cleansing space, item, or person is 100% pointless if you are doing it in a closed area. You are trying to shoo away the negative energy, making sense that the vibes must have somewhere else to go. Babe, open a window so all that lousy juju can escape. In fact, open as many windows and doors as possible.

Sage cleansing 101

Gather your items...

Sage smudge stick,

candle,

matches or lighter,

fireproof dish (I use a shell, but it does get hot),

crystals if you would like to use them in your ritual.

Light the candle and hold the fatter end of the smudge stick in the flames until it begins to smoke and smoulder. Remember the idea is to create smoke, don't burn the whole thing, or light it on fire as it begins to smoke. Take three deep breaths, let the smoke swirl around you and cleanse your energy ...

Cleansing your body/person

if your aim is to cleanse yourself, move the smudge stick around your body, allowing yourself to be enveloped in the cleansing smoke. Give it a go babe and let me know how you feel ....

Clear that negative stagnant energy from your money receiving areas

Our money receiving areas can hold a lot of trauma and negative energy. To cleanse your "money areas" and get rid of negative money vibes, do the same thing ... Grab your wallet, clean it out (yes, that means it's time to throw out those manky receipts and that spare condom you have had since 1992) and douse it in the cleansing smoke. Do the same with any physical items that you would hold money energy around, like your computer for online banking, your phone for checking your bank app, your small change jar, or your piggy bank filled with coins your nanna used to give you. CLEANSE IT ALL because it is time to create space and good energy for your money to flow into!!!!

Cleansing your home

If your goal is to cleanse the house, this is where you can begin to walk around and cleanse your space. Pay special attention to doorways, windows, corners of rooms, beds, etc. anywhere where energy may stagnate. You can wave and direct the smoke with your hands or use a feather if you like, but basically .... get it swirling. If you feel called to express the energy release verbally, you can say something like "negative energy you are cast out, be gone, there is only space for light and love in this home." Or if you are like me ... you are sage cleansing while you have beats cranked, whiskey in one hand and chanting "bad vibes, get fucked, fuck off." Once you are done, make sure to blow out the candle, and snuff out the smudge stick by pushing and dabbing it into your fireproof dish. That way, it will be ready to use next time.

Ta-da

Sage smudging is that simple, nothing to be afraid of.

MEDITATION + MANIFESTATION

I've said it before and I'll repeat it, Meditation SAVED ME!

Legit, I shudder to think of who I would have been today had I not found meditation. Meditation has helped me work through money demons, anxiety, eating disorder recovery, and allowed me to manifest the dream life I have today.

I've meditated my entire life, for as long as I can remember it's been a part of my day, my sleep routines, how I recenter and ground myself, even as a child, I would lie in bed and meditate, telling my feet it's time to sleep, then my ankles, then my legs and all the way up my body until I finally fell asleep.

Therefore, I'm excited to share this with you, but I also know not everyone loves meditation as much as I do ...

Reading this, you will probably be feeling one of two ways:

Number one _ *"yAASSs, meditation, I love meditation, here let me tell you about my favourite tracks, and my most profound insights, let's meditate now, LOVE IT."*

Or number two - *"ah, not another self-help bitch preaching on about meditation, I just can't do it, I've tried, and it doesn't work for me ... skip, NOPE, next chapter, please."*

Both ways are ok, and both approaches are normal... and even I have gone through both these in different points of my life.

If you already LOVE meditation, you will love this section, but if you are a bit hesitant, I want to ask you to trust me and open your heart and mind ... meditation might be exactly what you're looking for.

Many people struggle hardcore with meditation because they believe it must be all dead silence in a quiet room sitting cross-legged with incense. But that's not true. Sure, that's the way some people prefer to do it, and good for them, but others prefer to meditate while they walk, in the bath, lying on their bed as they go to sleep, or even just sitting in their car for those few precious moments the kids are still asleep in the driveway.

Meditation doesn't have to be silent. You can meditate to trance music or a guided meditation, and you could even listen to nature noises. If you have struggled with meditation before now, it just means you maybe haven't found the right style or way of doing meditation for you ... yet.

You may have noticed that every single offering of mine comes with at least one meditation included. this should be a good indication of how important meditation is to me and to my client's mindset and results. The intention and energy matter. What you wear, how you do it, or where you do it ... doesn't matter. It is about bringing yourself back to the centre, relaxing your body, and calming your mind.

Meditating your way to more Money

This book, my Elite membership, and this community is not the place for shame, guilt, or perfection ... meditation is where you accept yourself entirely as you are and show a little compassion for yourself.

Meditation can become the perfect tool for visualisation, which is vital for manifesting. Building an image in mind can be difficult for some, but it becomes much easier when you are in a meditative state. Whether you are building the mental image yourself or using a guided program to help navigate you into your imagination's depths, the idea is that meditation allows you to focus on your desired image without distraction (or without mental distraction, because sometimes the kids are still noisy AF).

Meditation, even on its most basic level, allows the mind to quiet. This prompts your natural frequency to rise as your mind moves away from anything that bothered you.

Abraham Hicks is a huge advocate for using meditation to get into what he calls "the receiving mode." To fully understand this, let's touch on energy flow again. Energy moves through us in two different directions. Let's call it the 'input' and the 'output'. When you are in 'output' mode, you emit energy out to the universe, whether that be via thought energy, emotional energy, or energy generated from your actions.

When you are in 'input mode' (otherwise known as the receiving mode), you are pulling energy inward, recharging the battery. There are no thoughts during meditation, there is nothing being emitted from you at all. There is just silence and stillness. Compared to a life where we are continually outputting (especially as mothers and business owners), those few moments where we can stop the output flow become almost euphoric. And it's during this stillness, that you naturally begin to draw energy in.

Tap into your inner rich babe....

So, what kinds of things might you 'receive' during the receiving mode?

Things like inspired guidance, clearer sight of which path you need to take ... or some people even communicate with spirit guides, the universe, or angels during this practice.

You will begin to magnetize your desires towards yourself every time you 'let go' of persistent thought. It is about creating a mental space for the new, exciting, and aligned to come into it. Meditation is essentially a quick and easy way to reach the high vibration required to shift you out of the 'asking mode' and into the 'receiving mode.'

In other words,

The more often you meditate and recharge yourself, the faster your desires can manifest into your life.

My top tips for magnetising meditation

- Find a tiny moment of calm. Sit or lie down, and if you can, close your eyes and start to breathe deeply, feel your body, feel your feet on the floor, or your body on the surface ... ground yourself through your breaths and allow your mind to centre.

- If you have trouble meditating in silence and find your thoughts running away and beginning to mentally prepare a shopping list or wondering about a school permission form ... that's probably a good indication that you would benefit from a guided meditation.

- You don't have to meditate in the same space every day. Yes, you might have your regular go-to spot, but trust me, there is nothing more exhilarating than meditating in a new place. That may be a beautiful park, on a mountain after a hike, an incredibly beautiful beach patch, or in your back yard basking in the full moon. Get creative, trust your intuition, and circulate energy by shaking up your routine.

- Don't sit cross-legged if you don't think it's comfortable. It is just not necessary. Forget the stereotypical images of people sitting cross-legged to meditate; ain't nobody got time for that if it only results in a numb leg. For most people, that position can be uncomfortable, not to mention distracting. What's most important is to find the meditation position that's most comfortable for YOU

- Get comfortable with discomfort. You are not alone, and you can't fuck this up. Rookies who are new to meditation, and even people like me who have been doing it for years — often experience negative emotions like panic, fear, restlessness, and irritation during a practice. Rather than trying to resist these emotions, please give them your full attention and allow them to come and go with neutrality. Over time the mind learns to recognise these emotions but gets used to putting a quick stop to any negative downward spiral. This is a skill that can be enormously beneficial, not only during meditation but also in daily life.

After your meditation practice, take a moment and check-in with yourself. Notice how you feel physically, emotionally, and mentally.

Are you calmer than you were before?

Does your mind feel clearer?

Do you feel more connected to your intuition?

The more you're able to establish a connection between your meditation practice and feeling better, the more invested you'll be in finding time to sit down each day to meditate.

Let's Meditate

I've created THIS meditation track specifically to help you envision and step into the feelings of wealth. I hope this meditation can show you how powerful manifesting through meditation can be.

Meditation can help you tap into a higher vibration of calm, peace, detachment, and alignment ... this energy is a POWERFUL magnet for more money.

The more often you can tap into this energy, the more likely you will have a moment of clarity and inspired action. You can become more open to seeing opportunities, and your attitude becomes more favourable to people, experiences, and abundance.

CLICK HERE or copy and paste this link into your

browser https://soundcloud.com/shona-gates/money-for-mummy-meditation-visualisation/s-KpW19

Meditation that isn't meditation

What if I told you meditating didn't just have to be "meditating"?

Meditation can essentially be anything that puts you in a high vibe, flow-based state. You know the feeling I'm talking about, the one where you feel connected to yourself and to source, where you are completely present in the moment, and embracing life with the playfulness that it inspires in us.

That "flow" state is different for each of us. But here is some of my favourite ways to meditate without meditating ...

- Listening to music and dancing around with no inhibitions,
- Colouring in an adult colouring book (or even kids' books),
- Going for a walk in nature and listening to just the rise and fall of your own breath or the steady beat of your feet on the pavement or path.

Why don't you try some "non" meditation today and see how it feels?

CHAPTER
9

DECLUTTERING – RELEASING TO RECEIVE

Living in a small house, decluttering and minimalism became a forced part of my life ....

However, over the years I've noticed a direct link to not only my happiness but also my feelings of abundance when I create space and order in my life.

At the beginning it was necessary ... now it's my way of life, and in this chapter I want to dive into not only my own experience, but also WHY decluttering is such an important part of your manifesting work.

Minimalism and manifestation

It's kind of like getting a haircut, they say a woman who is about to cut her hair is about to change her life, but for me decluttering signifies that change more than anything.

With a haircut we physically cut away the dead hair, the extra weight, the stuff holding us down, the tangled ends and knots that leave us feeling bedraggled and messy. Once we remove them, we feel lighter, bouncier, more confident, shinier ... ready to take on the world.

I feel that same way when I've done a thorough clean out and my house is filled with black plastic bags bound for the donation bin.

A new hair cut can allow us to step into the woman and life we are designing. A shiny sleek bob as you begin your law degree, or long carefree lioness curls as you step fully into the traveling boho babe you always wanted to be.

Blond, brunette, pink, or teal ... it's about stepping into and manifesting the new, true US.

But your shiny new bob doesn't just magically appear the moment you pin it on Pinterest, you must do the inspired action ... you have to call the salon, book the appointment, show up, express your desires/goals clearly and then use the aftercare.

And this example, I hope, seamlessly ties into our manifestation/decluttering topic...

There's a tangible relationship between decluttering and manifesting the life we desire.

Clutter and disorganisation make us feel overwhelmed, stressed out, and triggered. It exposes us to a lot of insignificant stimuli, causing our senses, especially as diffused aware women, to go into overload. Clutter takes our attention away from things we should focus on.

It makes it more difficult for us to relax mentally and physically and sends signals to our brains that our work is never finished (you know the feeling mumma). Sometimes you even may feel guilty and embarrassed for not being more organised, constantly battering yourself for not "getting it together".

Messy homes and workspaces leave us feeling anxious, helpless, and overwhelmed. The clutter is simply the external outside manifestation of how we've become cluttered in other areas of life. Clutter can also look like physical pain, or unhealthy, unfulfilling relationships, addictive behaviours, and mental chaos. These feelings and behaviours can have a negative impact on our energy, our attitude, and our productivity.

So, what does the universe think about clutter ....?

When our life is cluttered, unorganised, and in general a mess, but we are saying affirmations, and sage cleansing our clutter... you can see how it's kind of sending the wrong message.

This is what the universe says …. (In a calm Beyoncé voice, because in my head that's exactly what the universal intelligence sounds like)

- THE UNIVERSE - *"hmm, well she says she wants a boyfriend to come into her life, but look around this girl's home, there isn't a spare inch of closet space in sight and her bathroom counter couldn't fit another moisturiser on it … she hasn't got the space in her life for a boyfriend even if she wanted one"*

- THE UNIVERSE - *"oh honey, all the "I am a rich wealthy woman" affirmations in the world aren't going to help you while you are still hoarding clothes that you haven't worn in 8 years … if you truly felt abundant, you wouldn't feel the need to hold onto things "just in case"".*

- THE UNIVERSE - *"I want to give your new car to you sooo bad babe, but girl, you must not really believe I can do it, because your garage is packed full of old Christmas decorations and you're still driving around in your POS Honda, and girl it's filthy, you haven't even got it ready to sell .... I don't know if you're ready for this brand new range rover manifestation that I've got sitting here waiting for you"*

- THE UNIVERSE - *"you've got minimalist home décor pins all over Pinterest, and yet you keep putting off sorting out your home until your "next house" and stepping over piles of crap left right and centre. Girl, I have the next home sitting here waiting to show up for you (and its EPIC), but you got to show me you are ready for that next level. Sort your shit out in this home and level UP yourself, then you're going to be ready for this EPIC joana-gaines-esqu masterpiece I have ready for you."*

Are you feeling it? ... can you see how it looks from the perspective of universal intelligence?

What do you think the universe would be noticing about your life in terms of what you're trying to manifest right now?

Remember clutter can be both physical and mental ....

I was honestly really confused when chapters in one of the minimalism books I read spent time sharing about health, fitness, eating habits, grooming and relationships … "I thought I was getting a book about owning less stuff" I wondered to myself, but after I had read and fully absorbed the entire book, it made sense. Decluttering and condensing are both external and internal, physical, and mental … It's about all of it.

Like my grandpa used to say to me, *"the way you do anything is the way you do everything"*

Ask yourself these questions …. and be honest in your answers just like in the self-care chapter.

Am I eating right?

Am I getting the exercise I want?

Am I getting enough rest?

Do I take time for a regular spiritual practice?

Am I indulging in addictive behaviours?

Do I have a medical professional involved in my care?

Am I addressing health issues?

How am I managing stress and achieving work/life balance?

What needs to be eliminated so that I can step into my fully realised life?

What needs to be added?

With Love, release the people and situations that hold you back from your highest good. Take responsibility for forgiving those who have harmed you.

The space you clear by throwing out stuff that no longer serve you, creates space for clarity in other areas of life.

The universal law of vacuum ....

"The Law of The Vacuum states that all material forces of the universe abhor the vacuum and rush to fill each hole"

This Law states that space allows movement, and that when all space is filled, the solidarity prevents further movement or growth. By removing and reducing the unwanted and unnecessary part of one's life we can create the time, space, atmosphere, and opportunities to move, grow, replenish and to rebuild on a more solid foundation.

This Law creates the spaces in which you can place only the highest and only the best with the least amount of energy and expense.

Decluttering activates the law of attraction. One of the easiest and most effective ways to effortlessly attract something new into your life is to create some empty space. Once you create the space, the universe will try to fill it with that which you desire.

You all know this from personal experience when you've cleaned out a drawer in your dresser only to find it gets filled up with stuff almost before you know it.

Nature cannot resist an empty space.

This works for your schedule too. If you want more time, leave some blank space in your schedule, and start showing up 10 minutes early to every appointment. Don't book everything up solid so that there is no room for some new opportunity to come in.

If you're living in fear of lack and strangle, holding on to everything—your material possessions, your time, your love, your energy, or your ideas—you're shutting yourself off from the abundant flow of life. When you block up a stream, the water becomes stagnant, green and EWW. When you close off the flow of your life, you become stagnant.

The more unwanted things clutter your life, the less room there will be for the things you want to be able to appear, duh.

GUEST FEATURE -----

Decluttering with sally from @organisedbysally

I created Organised by Sally after spending time as a stay-at-home mum. I wanted to combine my passion for organising, with my love for helping and supporting others. My dream came about after a conversation with a good friend, she was often overwhelmed by mess and despite a desire to stay tidy, she didn't know where to start. From there I transformed an idea into a budding business, helping clients to declutter and organise their homes in a way they can maintain and that makes sense to them.

As a Professional Organiser I have learnt many things about clutter over the years. Here are some of the best tips I can give you about decluttering and organising your home.

#1 Concentrate on the right things

When it comes to decluttering, try and concentrate on keeping the things that add VALUE to your life instead of on what you want to get rid of. By doing this you are putting yourself into a positive mindset and it will allow you to let go of things that you really don't need. Ask yourself: Does this add value to my life? Does it 'spark joy'?

Do I actually use this item? Trust your judgement, you know what is best for you and your family.

#2 Start small

It is easy to get overwhelmed when it comes to clearing clutter from your life, especially if it has been building for a long time. My suggestion is to set yourself some small achievable tasks and build your decluttering muscles e.g., clear a shelf in your bathroom cabinet or sort out your bedside table. As you get more confident, you can start tackling bigger projects. If you need to, use a timer to keep yourself motivated and on track.

#3 Plugging the holes

Have you ever been in the situation where you have decluttered and organised only for things to go back to the way it was? Or worse?! One of the main reasons this is happening is because you haven't plugged the clutter holes. Think of your house like it's a boat, if you have holes in the hull, clutter is just going to keep sinking your ship until you do something about it. - Look at your shopping habits - Talk to your family and friends about the changes you are trying to make - Go paperless and unsubscribe from all those promotional emails trying to sell you stuff - When it comes to gifts, ask for experiences (movie tickets, massage voucher) and consumables (e.g., chocolates, magazines, flowers). Making changes like these can have a big impact on the amount of stuff that flows into your home. And if it never enters your home, you never have to deal with it!!

Bonus tip: clutter is sneaky. Once you have made your decision to let it go, remove it from your house ASAP! Otherwise, it'll just creep its way back in. Trust me.

x Sally

VISUALISATION

Visualisation, like so many things in this book, really boils down to playing pretend and tricking your body and brain into really, truly believing something is possible for you.

We manifest effectively by keeping our sights on who we want to become and how we want to feel (note how I didn't say "what you want to buy"). Manifestation is simply the process of calling in the right vibration of what we want to embody. We do this by visualising the version of us that has already achieved it.

By asking ourselves how it feels in our physical body, cognitively, energetically, emotionally, and spiritually?

For example, for a long time I visualised and scripted on my perfect day, one where I wake up feeling energised, connected to my husband, supported, adored, surrounded by love, adventure, and fun. Before I would go to bed at night I would envision my perfect day, waking up early, having a moment with my husband before the kids woke up, feeling confident and connected, etc.

What this was doing was tapping me into the vibrations and feelings as if the perfect day had already happened. Sitting in that vibration signalled to my subconscious that this feeling and state is my truth, my reality. Very quickly my reality shifted to match up with my visualisation.

For any of you guys who don't know, I have a side hobby, it's not one I scream from the rooftops, but it's also not one I hide...

I write erotic fiction, erotic fantasy fiction, Smut, clit-erature whatever you want to call it.

It's not something you can publicly read ... yet (shhh that book is in the works too), but nevertheless I spend a lot of time thinking about writing and scripting out various sex scenes, dialog, and erotic situations.

Often a day or two after writing a particularly steamy scene, it happens in my reality, and it still shocks me. Not the act itself, that is beyond delightful .... but there is always this moment when I'm like *"wait is this happening"* and afterwards I find myself asking my husband if he's been reading my book drafts, because often he has re-enacted that scene EXACTLY, without even knowing what it was.

And every time he is as shocked as I am, he doesn't have the faintest clue I had been literally daydreaming about this exact scenario not 1-2- days earlier, he hates reading and he wouldn't even know how to find them on my laptop to know what I have written in the first place, and yet something just convinces him to try this new thing, idea, position, phrase.

These scenes go from my imagination to my reality in rapid succession.

IF there was ever any proof that detailed, specific, emotionally charged visualisation works

…. This is it. My sex life. Haha.

In every single book I've ever read about cultivating a positive mindset, law of attraction, or manifestation, a key part of the book speaks on the power of visualisation.

This excerpt from *Kevin L. Michel, Moving Through Parallel Worlds To Achieve Your Dreams: The Epic Guide To Unlimited Power (pp. 117-121). Michel Leadership. Kindle Edition.* Is exceptionally powerful, so rather than re-create the wheel, I wanted to reference it here as an easy guide to visualisation.

How To Visualize:

1. Sit down comfortably in a place where you will not be disturbed for 10 minutes (set an alarm to alert you when your time is up – a song, as an alarm, is best).
2. Decide specifically what success or achievement you want to visualize.
3. If available, view a picture of the environment where this achievement takes place (for example a picture of the Serengeti or a picture of your workplace).
4. Close your eyes.
5. Slow your breathing by taking very deep breaths. Consciously take control of and monitor your breathing.
6. Imagine your body relaxing, one major body part at a time from top to bottom: Head, shoulders, arms, legs then feet.
7. Keep breathing deeply. Imagine each body part more relaxed than before.
8. Imagine yourself in the environment with as much detail as you can create (As with all things, practice makes perfect – you can even visualize yourself visualizing to get better at this :-))
9. Awake when your music starts (or timer goes off). Acknowledge your awesomeness.

With practice, your visualizations will become more real and even your conscious mind will be momentarily startled when you awake. When you get to that point where even your conscious mind gets sucked into the illusion, your focus and motivation will increase exponentially. This is the point where the two parts of your mind have aligned, albeit temporarily.

At this point you start to operate with a level of grace, confidence, and unflappability that leads you to do exactly what you need to do, exactly when you need to do it. It is a very powerful state of continuous flow, that if maintained, sheds light on your path and enlightens your soul.

Kevin L. Michel, Moving Through Parallel Worlds To Achieve Your Dreams: The Epic Guide To Unlimited Power (pp. 117-121). Michel Leadership. Kindle Edition.

Let's make a vision board

Under my big sexy adult bed, with mature olive-colored sheets and a fancy throw pillow, you will find a black plastic box.

And no, it's not full of kinky stuff, you dirty-minded pervert ... (that's another box).

This one is filled to the brim with my diaries, journals, and scrap books from the past 30 years. Full of dreams, high school crushes, "Shona loves Aaron 4 ever" scrawled into many of them, clipped out magazine photos, wedding dress pictures, haircuts, and secret notes. Even though rereading some of them makes me cringe, makes me sad for the broken girl that I was, most serve as a reminder that everything I have in my life today, began here ... as a desire, a dream, and a wish.

Everything I have ever manifested, called into my life, or achieved began on my vision board/scrapbooks/dream wish lists. Things like my dream car, my laptop, my watch, my sexy husband, (yes, I even vision boarded him too) and even my journey as a mother and businesswoman.

It all started with some scissors, magazines, and a glue stick ... sitting down and creating intentional time in my life to focus on my goals, what I wanted, and visualising it was always one of the first steps on my journey to actually achieving it.

And that's why I LOVE running my annual vision board parties.

However, time and time again, I see comments on Facebook posts or DMs hitting my inbox and people reaching out to me on social media who live in other states/countries asking, *"How do I make a vision board?"*

So, it's time to take this vision board party from my back yard to around the world. I have taken my entire vision board process and packaged it up in this awesome section for you, so I can guide you step by step through the process I use no matter where you are in the world.

If you think vision boards are bogus, then the joke is on you.

They work, and there is actually a really simple explanation for why they work so well. Creating a sacred space that displays what you want, actually does bring it to life, because we know, what we focus on expands. When you create a vision board and place it in a space you see it often, you essentially end up doing short visualisation exercises throughout the day.

How to create a vision board ...

Visualization is one of the most powerful mind exercises you can do. According to the popular book The Secret, "The law of attraction is forming your entire life experience and it is doing that through your thoughts. When you are visualizing, you are emitting a powerful frequency out into the Universe." Whether you believe that or not, we know that visualization works.

Olympic athletes have been using it for decades to improve performance and Psychology Today reported that the brain patterns activated when a weightlifter lifts heavy weights are also similarly activated when the lifter just imagined (visualized) lifting weights. So, what's the big secret to creating a vision board that works?

It's simple: Your vision board should focus on how you want to feel, not just on things that you want. But don't get me wrong, it's great to include the material stuff too.

However, the more your board focuses on how you want to feel, the more it will come to life. There is only one major rule to creating a vision board that works, and it's that there aren't any rules.

You aren't going to mess it up, you can create your vision board on your own terms.

Vision boarding your way to more money

- STEP 1. SET THE MOOD - Some calming music, a few girlfriends, wine, some candles, incense, a quiet place, or maybe even meditating first ... whatever floats your boat and gets you in the zone, do that ... do not attempt to do this while studying for an exam or making school lunches, this is you time, set time aside, do it properly.

- STEP 2. GET YOUR S**T TOGETHER - Gather your supplies, magazines, printed images from your multiple fantasy Pinterest boards, scissors, glue, glitter, post cards, photos, badass motivational quotes, ... and of course the board ... it doesn't literally have to be a board, you can use a piece of card, a pin board, a photo frame, or the entire wall in your bedroom ... whatever suits you ... go for it!

- STEP 3. SET YOUR GOALS - Sometimes that can be the overwhelming bit. I find the easiest way is this exercise bellow ... set a timer for 5 minutes ...pretend that you are 5 and this piece of paper is magic, literally anything you write down will appear or happen to you .... there is no judgement, there is no should, just start writing, let it all flow out be as messy or as neat as you like, there is NO wrong answers .... Ok go....***Tap into your inner rich babe......***

- STEP 4. COLLECT VISUAL REPRESENTATIONS OF YOUR GOALS - And get specific, for example if you want to make 200k this year, print yourself a bank slip and fill it out paying yourself 200k, if you want to own a white range rover, print it off.... You know the one with the super-hot rims, print it honey .... if you want to complete a marathon, print off the logo or pictures of the people at the finish line, or if you've always wanted to visit Bora Bora, go online, plan the holiday, and print off the pictures of the most amazing hotel you're going to stay at one day ... GET SPECIFIC AND HAVE FUN. ***Get them goals baby.......***

- STEP 5. CREATE A COLLAGE - It doesn't have to be pretty or perfect, heck it doesn't even have to make sense to anyone else ... this is JUST for you!

- STEP 6. HANG IT UP - Preferably some where you are going to see it multiple times a day. So, your bedroom wall when you wake up, your office, your fridge, the back of your toilet door, basically where you are going to see it the most. Make sure you spend a moment each day looking at your vision board truly visualizing and feeling how amazing it will be when you have achieved it all!!! FEEL IT ALL!

- STEP 7. START WORKING TOWARDS THOSE GOALS HONEY!!!

My top tips for a vision board THAT WORKS

- Your vision board is YOUR vision board. It is only for YOU. It doesn't have to be on brand, match your colours, or make sense to anyone but YOU. So just do what feels good babe, as the very wise Taylor swift once said, "haters gonna hate, just shake it off, shake it off".

- If the glue and glitter scrap book style isn't for you, that's TOTALLY ok (it's not for me either these days). Jump online to Canva and use stock images or some Pinterest ones to create a vision board that you love, then simply download and print - tada, no glue gun burns here.

- Vision boards don't just have to be on the wall or the back of your toilet door, think about using the things/devices you are on the most, like your phone and computer and even the tv screen saver, instead of a boring lock screen, or a photo of your puppy, why don't you make the most of that subliminal reprogramming and turn your vision board into your screensaver. Saturate your brain with the goals until they feel so real to you that your faith is unshakeable.

THE POWER OF AFFIRMATIONS AND POSITIVE THOUGHTS

Affirmations work. They work because we are speaking instructions to the universe and co creating our dream reality. But they also work because of science, brains and all that psychology stuff.

I used to feel like a ginormous self-obsessed twat, standing Infront of my mirror repeating *"money loves to be in my life, I am healthy, wealthy, and successful".*

I didn't believe it, I was saying abundant phrases, but my bank account was in the minus figures, it felt wrong like a liar and false. But I knew that the pessimistic attitude was what had gotten me in this toxic save, binge, panic pattern with money in the first place. I owed it to myself, and my family, and even my future, to try something different, to get a bit uncomfortable and do something NEW.

Same + same = same

It was up to me to be the change, to choose differently, to create the new reality I desired.

I still felt like a twat, for the first few months, but I stuck to it and eventually I stopped feeling self-conscious and started believing the words I was saying. When I could believe it, that's when I achieved it. But don't worry it's not all spiritual voodoo, its science, and it works!

As much as I'm a spiritual girl, with her crystals, sage and orgasmic manifestation, I'm equal parts highly logical, I devour documentaries on Astrophysics as if they are skittles, obsess over science, and binge out on psychology articles. I research what I speak about, I aim to understand everything from both a spiritual and a scientific approach.

Our thoughts, actions, and emotions are all so interlinked, they all affect each other.

What we think about consciously has a direct effect on the actions we take every day,

"I'm thinking about my family, so I call my mum"

What we feel has a direct effect on the actions we take,

"I miss my mum; I think I'll call her"

And the actions we take can affect our feelings,

"I called my mum today, after I spoke to her, I felt really great"

Another example is how a thought (not necessarily a fact) can change our emotions and behaviours.

"The doorbell rings"

Thought – *"ohh I hope it's my food delivery"*

Action - bounce to the door smiling and ready

Emotion – anticipation, excitement, happiness, hunger

"The doorbell rings"

Thought – *"I wasn't expecting anyone, I wonder who it could be"*

Action – move to the door carefully and quietly check the peephole

Emotion – caution, anticipation, wariness

It's kind of like a triangle, each corner is important in supporting the balance. Why is this important? It's important because once we understand the connection here, it's then that we can begin to change our future.

When we decide there is a certain aspect of our life we would like to change, we can take 3 different approaches:

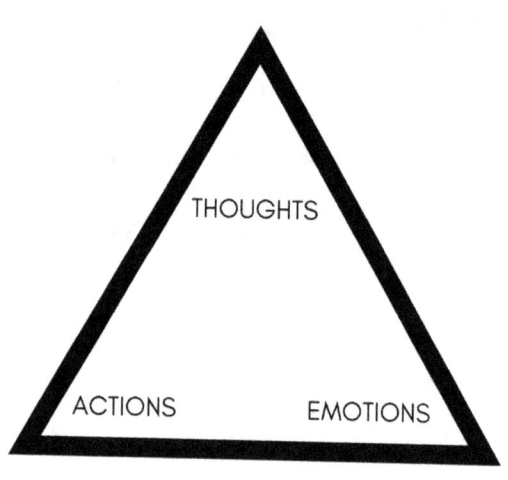

Some are easier to change than others, for example, trying to shift an emotion is a lot harder and takes quite a fair amount of practice to be able to shift out of a negative feeling into a positive one without also using thoughts and actions.

Let's use the example of wanting to wake up earlier ...

If you decide to shift your ACTIONS first ... you could set an alarm for 5 minutes earlier each day until you achieve your desired wake time, you could set out your clothes for the next day or put your coffee machine on a time to help it become easier to get up and going. You could take action by going to bed earlier or moving your phone/alarm to the bathroom or out of reach, so you have to physically leave your bed to turn it off. All of these are powerful changes you can make.

Adding in THOUGHTS to this scenario increases your likelihood of success even more so. Don't allow yourself to slip back into thoughts of *"ahh I miss sleep-ins"*, *"I'm so tired"*, *"I hate waking up in the morning"* ... all that does is reaffirm the same tired cycle you've been stuck in. Affirming positive thoughts like *"I wake up early"*, *"I am an early riser"*, *"I love my fresh morning starts"*, *"I feel powerful when I start my day early"*, etc., etc.

By affirming your new choice over and over again, it becomes your new truth, your new reality, and combined with actions, thoughts will begin to change your emotions ... you might not feel *"powerful"* the first morning you stumble out of bed at 6am.... But you can bet that after the first 3-4 weeks when your alarm goes off, you will begin to feel as powerful as you have been affirming all along.

Words have so much power.

Affirmations combined with actions can shift our emotions. it's how we succeed.

Each of them affects all of them.

In this section I wanted to share some of my favourite and most powerful abundant affirmations that I use every single day and I have written on post-it notes and stuck them around my house and set as reminders in my phone. These are the affirmations that have come through my heart and my soul's work, and I use them every single day. You may or may not have heard them in other places and I certainly don't claim to have created any of this, but this is just what flowed through me in my journaling practice, and these affirmations are what I use to step into my abundance every day.

You might like to write these out or journal on them or you might like to stick them up on post-it notes or set one as a reminder in your phone every day... whatever you decide to do with them just know that they are here for you to use in whichever way feels best.

I am worthy of an abundant and wealthy life.

My work is of high value and worthy of HUGE compensation.

I am supported by a kind and loving universe.

This always gets to work for me.

I am worthy and enough just because I exist.

The more pleasure I feel the more money I make.

Everything is always working out for me.

I am worthy of all I have and all I deserve.

I am deserving of love, money, and success.

Money comes my way with ease.

It's not happening to me; it's happening for me and the greater good.

I am sexy and spiritual at the same time.

I choose NOW to receive all that is meant for me.

I am a badass visionary worthy of massive abundance.

I get to decide that life gets to be easy.

My soul is always leading me through the path of least resistance.

I am honoured, respected, supported, and desired for my gifts, talents, and abilities.

I always get what I want, and this is a good thing.

Fun like Friday night and easy like Sunday morning every day.

I get to feel honoured and desired in all things, all the time.

My success is inevitable, and everything is always working out for me.

I am incapable of messing up what is already mine and what has always been meant for me.

Every day in every way I am becoming richer and richer.

I am worthy of all my desires, and my work and myself is ENOUGH.

Money loves me and I love money.

It is always mother fucking working out for me.

I get to have everything…. Absolutely everything.

I am love, I am wealth, I am perfection just as I am.

HELLO ABUNDANCE

It is safe for me to go BIG and play full out.

Everything I touch turns to mother fucking GOLD.

It gets to be easy, and I get to have everything I want in its fullest version.

I am worthy of all good things; abundance is always freely flowing to me.

My success is absolutely inevitable, and I am always on the right track.

Abundance is my natural state, and I am worthy of all my desires.

What I want is valid and matters.

I am love and receive love every day.

I am good enough as I am, and everything is always working out for me.

I am bold, passionate, purposeful, and always live in flow with my higher self.

I have everything I need when I need it.

The universe is always working in my favour and bringing me everything I need.

I am a money making badass.

Money is my best friend, and she loves to show up and surprise me in different ways.

I decide that making money gets to be super easy, it gets to be FUN.

I always live in a rich and abundant life.

I choose to drop the mother fucking struggle and the drama around money.

Making and manifesting LOTS of money is my new normal

Money flows to me every single day in expected and unexpected ways as if like magic.

It is impossible for me to not make money, everything I do makes me money.

People love to pay me and are excited to pay me.

I fully trust and decide to be fully supported and loved by the universe.

The world benefits from me becoming a wealthy woman.

I am breaking the cycle of being broke for my family.

I am open and receptive to all the wealth life offers me.

HELLO ABUNDANCE

I am a magnet for prosperity, abundance, and financial blessings.

I am thankful for all the opportunities and experiences that money gives me.

Every dollar I spend comes back to me multiplied.

Thankyou universe for the money that's flowing into my bank account.

My actions create constant prosperity.

I am open to money coming into my life in new ways I never even imagined before.

You are enough today. You were enough yesterday. You will be enough tomorrow.

I will thrive on trust, faith, and uncertainty.

I know and believe that the more I release and detach the more miracles and money that come into my life.

Every day I am operating out of a state of abundance and total overflow.

Every cell in my body is a perfect vibrational match for my desires.

Wealth and abundance are my birth right, I claim it for myself and my family NOW.

It is safe for me to be a rich and powerful woman.

I manifest abundance by being grateful for what I already have.

I don't need others to validate me because I fucking love myself fully and completely.

I am full of money-making ideas that effortlessly turn into cash.

I release every block that held me back from receiving prosperity.

The whole universe and the world are conspiring to make sure I am prosperous. I cannot fail.

I have the power to manifest ANYTHING I desire!

My favourite way to use affirmations is verbal, but you can absolutely use these as written intentions for your day, just as visual reminders, or even phrases that you just say in context. Every time I spend money, I remind myself *"there's always more where this comes from"*, every time I invest in my business, I'm reminding myself that *"I believe that every dollar I spend comes back to me multiplied"*, and you will find the more you use these affirmations the more they just become a new part of your lifestyle.

It's all part of rewiring your relationship and your mindset towards money.

Choosing abundance over scarcity and love over fear every day.

Bridging affirmations

Sometimes the gap between being a broke bitch and affirming *"I am a millionaire badass"* just feels too big, too vast, too insurmountable. That's where we can use bridging affirmations, to stay in our power and truth while tapping into the inner wealthy woman.

if *"I'm financially empowered and independent"* feels too much like a lie, start with *"I am open and willing to learn more about wealth every single day"*.

If *"money is my best friend and loves being in my life"* feels too much like a lie, start with *"every day I am nurturing and healing my relationship with money"*.

If *"I am a money making badass"* feels too strong, begin with *"I am open to receiving more money into my life from expected and unexpected ways"*

Sometimes manifestation and using the law of attraction will happen to us in this huge way, manifesting our soul mate, or winning the lottery, but often it happens in small, wonderful ways, like a free coffee, a stranger topping up your parking meter, a friend lending you a book, or an invitation to an event. So, if you need to start small, start small, it's ok.

In your own way, in your own time.

CHAPTER 12

ANGEL NUMBERS + SIGNS FROM THE UNIVERSE

Here is the thing, I trust myself and my intuition fully.

I know inside I don't need permission, validation, or approval from any outside source to follow my heart and stay aligned with me and my path. However, I'm not above admitting that getting a little confirmation from the universe every now and again is reassuring as hell.

When I seek a "sign" from the universe, it's not often to help me decide, or receive guidance, for me, it's more of a little high-five from the universe that I'm on the right path, that I am staying true to my heart and headed in the right direction.

Some people look for signs in words, animals, symbols, etc. and that's awesome, you do you girl.

For me it's in numbers, and it always has been.

For as long as I can remember, I've noticed 11.11.

At school, in maths, at home, on the microwave, in license plates, building numbers, and homework. It just kept showing up, but it wasn't until I was an adult, that I googled it years ago and figured out what it meant, like the sage cleansing showing up in my life again, it felt like home.

And once again I reconnected with that little baby witch inside me that saw beyond the logic of the world and probed further into the spiritual workings of the universe. Angel numbers or repeating numbers as you may know them are simply signs that you are in alignment, that you are on the right path. It's the universe sending you a little fist bump to let you know you are not alone, and that it has your back.

If you constantly see the same numbers over and over again chances are it's not a coincidence and is actually a sign from the universe.

Since I get asked for this so often, here is my little **Angel number cheat sheet.**

111

Your desires are manifesting quickly. Get your ducks in a row because it's about to happen FAST.

222

Breathe. Stop freaking the fuck out, stop worrying things are going your way. It's all according to plan.

333

Peace, joy, divinity. A sign of your true purpose and your soul work in action.

444

The ultimate angel number. It's a sign that your guides are with you, that you are not alone on your soul's mission.

555

Change is on the horizon, BIG UPLEVEL, get ready to say goodbye to what no longer serves you.

666

Not the devil's number. This is a sign from the universe to reset and recalibrate. Get back on path.

777

Lady luck is on your side, super spiritual alignment. Stay true to yourself and take advantage of opportunities.

888

MAJOR MONEY MANIFESTATION abundance is on its way, keep your energy and gratitude HIGH.

999

Indicates the completion of an energetic cycle. Finishing a chapter, a project, this is about moving on to NEW.

Timing

The angel number's timing is also no coincidence. Noticing the context of when they show up. What's happening in those moments? Were you thinking about something specific? Did something happen before or after? Noticing those details can provide clues to the number's meaning. I kept noticing a lot of 222 popping up in my life. But it wasn't until I paid attention to the timing that I noticed a pattern, around the end of the month I would start to feel anxious about hitting my income goals, and the inevitable 0 as my reports clear out at the EOM and I start again trying to hit my income goals. The 222 number that kept showing up on my watch, microwave, oven, invoices, and bank account was trying to remind me to Breathe, stop freaking the fuck out, stop worrying if things are going your way. It's all according to plan.

Combination Numbers

"What if I keep seeing 11.22? what does that mean?"

I have often been asked this by the girls in my Elite membership because it can leave us feeling a little stumped? because the numbers are not repeating am I just imagining it or seeking signs where there are not any? let me reassure you, it is a sign, but even if it wasn't, the fact that you are searching for a sign and looking for that reassurance and guidance... that is a sign in itself.

Any combination number is a STRONG sign that you are on the right track. But also look at the individual numbers for message and meaning.

What do I do about it?

Here is the thing, just knowing about them and sharing a screen shot of it on your Instagram story doesn't mean shit …. Sorry not sorry.

They are not just messages but rather calls to action. Implementing and acting on the pieces of wisdom angel numbers provide is how you can harness their power to improve your life, love, and abundant attraction. It's a fist bump, a high five, a keep on going girl you got this…. So, keep moving forward, keep taking inspired action. It's one thing to create the momentum and it's another thing to be ready to catch it.

RAISING YOUR WEALTH FREQUENCY

Otherwise known as becoming an energetic match for riches, raising your mother fucking prices, or ... the shift. The shift, from where you are now to where you will be.

The shift comes in many different forms, for many different people. What vibes for me might not for you. likewise, what makes my soul cringe might be your favourite thing ever. The point is, do it your way, and fucking own it. I'm just here as a guide, as your sat nav, you've told me the destination you want to arrive at, and now my job is to present you with different options/ routes so you can choose the one that you vibe with the most.

First, we are going to talk about the shift, which is really just stepping into the highest version of yourself .... then I'm going to break it down on how I become an energetic match of raising my prices and embodying the energy of *"people love to pay me"*.

THE SHIFT

Back in my MLM days, I created this alter, the ego, kind of like my superman that went into battle instead of Clark Kent. Battle .... Being the stage in front of 200 people, or a webinar with 400 people in the background. Little old "Shona" from the Barossa valley who was just a mum and felt massive imposter syndrome, was nervous standing in the backstage, but "badass shona/Sasha Fierce" she was excited, confident, she walked like a Victoria's secret model, her heels tall, her power blazer on, nails dark, and hair perfect, she walked on that stage like she mother fucking owned it.

Big smile, presentation clicker in hand, she would wave to the audience as the music cranked around her. And she fucking nailed it.

She was the next level me, and while I didn't feel like her on a Monday morning while my 2-year-old spat her weet-bix back at me, on that stage I stepped fully into her ... the more I played pretend, the more I affirmed that I was excited (rather than nervous) the more I walked the walk, talked the talk and believed in myself .... the more I became that version of me.

I stepped into the attitude of her, the thoughts of her, the actions she took, what she wore, how she spoke, her beliefs.

I played pretend with it.

I got dramatic.

I had fun with it and so can you.

So, let's talk about the next level you. The one who has it all, the one that has already made it to the top, she's confident, she's badass, she knows her shit, she feels totally abundant every day and lives from a place of total overflow .... you know what I'm talking about.

So how do we shift into that version, how do we vibe with it and tap into the feelings, thoughts, beliefs, and actions that come with it? it's different for everyone but here are a few ideas to try on for size.

- Picturing and imagining your new reality. Daydream your perfect life. A visualisation meditation allows you to get totally immersed in the vision behind your closed eyes, create an anchor with the meditation music that you can use to step into the visualisation each time.

- Use music to tap into a flow state when you align with the feelings and emotions you desire to tap into in your new reality. For me cranking my favourite jams on the drive to school run in the morning, is an instant vibe. I'm elevated, expansive, more open to opportunities, more resilient, energetic, confident, fun, playful and open. ***LINK PLAYLIST***

- Movement, now you won't ever catch me running these days, on purpose, but those of you who do and love running, will know the flow state I speak of. For some of us it's in downward dog pose during yoga, for me it's a hike, nature, no music, no phone, no one to chat with, just the sound of my feet hitting the dirt and my heart pumping. swimming, running, hiking, dancing … movement helps us tap into flow. It allows our subconscious to actually speak to us, to guide us, direct us, tap us back into what is true for us. This is the state in which as we circulate energy and movement, we can have huge internal shifts.

- Drama, when we were little, playing pretend came so easy to us, we were able to create an entire world from two cardboard tubes, a tiara, and a

Tupperware lid. It was so easy because we did it all day long, we weren't scared of being seen as silly, we were just creative balls of confidence, imagination, and pure messy magic. So go on, try having more imaginary conversations, full shower arguments, mirror work, playing dress-up, experimenting with new makeup, doing an "interview" with Forbes in your car on your way to work, or trying on accents to see which ones make you feel the most luxe.

- Dear diary, today was fucking amazing ... affirmations are great, affirmations work, but are you ready to step into the most powerful shift of all? ... Write down in your diary for the day as if you already have everything you desire, you have it all, you're the person you dream of being, journal on that in the past tense of "dear diary" and see how powerful it feels.

- "I am fully supported by the universe, nothing I do could fuck this up, my success is inevitable" for a lot of people (me included) thinking and speaking our new reality into existence is key ... when I had $358 to my name and my electricity bill was $356 ... I paid it, and as I swiped my card at the post office, I affirmed to myself out loud "there's always more where this comes from", now, I don't have to worry about bills, I always do have more than enough, way more than enough ... but I believed it, way back then, and I spoke it into existence before it was my reality.

At the end of the day, the how doesn't matter ... but the fact that you begin to feel and act differently because of the steps you are taking, that's what matters.

It's about sitting with it and really asking yourself if I had all the mother fucking money, if I drove my dream car, if my business hit 7 figures, if I got the promotion/dream job/pay rise, if I won the lottery, if I booked my dream client .... if I was in total overflow and abundance with wealth and money ...

what would I be feeling right now?

What would I be able to hear, see, smell, taste, touch?

What would I KNOW ... with full certainty about myself and my life, what would be my truth and energetically absolute for me?

What would I be seeing, thinking, feeling, believing if this was all my reality?

How would I treat myself? How would I speak to myself?

What thoughts would I believe?

When we begin to take a baby step of courage and begin acting, thinking, and feeling from this place of our highest millionaire self, we begin to literally create our new reality through inspired action. it becomes the new standard; it becomes normal for you. It becomes EASY, natural, and completely *"of course it is"*.

Set the new standard for yourself.

You are in charge of your future, you get to choose, and your reality is created by your thoughts, beliefs, and actions today ... so don't keep repeating the same version of yourself year after year or handing over your power to coaches, gurus, mentors, etc. when YOU are the only one who has the power to create this shift and move forwards.

You got this,

you're ready,

you're capable,

and it is all working out for you.

ALIGNED PRICING

The conversation around *"raise your prices, charge your worth"* is floating around everywhere. And yet no one is talking about *"energetically raising your prices"*.

IF we raise our prices without matching it energetically, the gap in our belief causes us to self-sabotage.

Early in my business, I was waaaay undercharging for my services, I lacked confidence, and every time I tried to pull my rates up to align it more with the industry standards, I felt myself hesitating. Even when I realised that at my current pricing, I was LOSING money, I still hesitated. When I finally bit the bullet and doubled my course pricing, I still found myself offering discounts, throwing in freebies, and even years of money mindset work didn't seem to help.

Because here is the thing, even though my pricing made sense, I didn't FEEL it, I didn't BELIEVE it, and at the end of the day I didn't fully feel worthy of it.

So, I invested and worked with a mentor to help me align with my prices, this is a method that changed EVERYTHING for me, and I've been teaching it ever since. BECAUSE IT MATTERS. Often When I'm working with a client one on one, we walk through their money story, take time to heal their relationship with money, but when it comes to asking for money, they get totally stuck.

Raising prices is a part of life, charging what you need to turn a profit, put food on the table, and live your life is necessary. But when we see it as this big scary new number, that's what creates the fear, the panic, the feelings of not deserving it. So how do we shift this ... we shift it by completely normalizing the number, we make it our new normal, our new average, so it feels comfortable, and our subconscious is no longer threatened.

So here is my process and some points I run through with clients,

raising your prices without energetically aligning with those prices create a discrepancy which we then self-sabotage to rectify.

You have to charge a price you can get behind and believe in it, there's no such thing as pricing to match your competitor, your heart and your intuition knows what price it should be, trust that. The minute I let go of the "marketing rule of $7, $47, $97, $197, etc." and just charged what the fuck I wanted, trust me babe, I sold a lot more. Just because someone else charges that, it doesn't mean you have to.

I align myself with my new pricing by immersing myself in the pricing, you can write it on post-it notes, put it everywhere, make it your screen saver, pop it on your bathroom mirror.

If actually voicing your prices or sending a quote to someone makes you break out in a sweat, use scripts, or an assistant to detach a bit from it. I create scripts in my phone notes where I say, "this is how much I charge per hour …", and this helps me detach emotionally and doesn't give me room to back down or offer discounts.

Vision board the pricing, what will your life look like once that is your new reality? How will it feel to confidentially own these prices?!

Set reminders as pretend payment notifications of your new amount. When I shifted my pricing, it really helped me to set an alarm 3 times a day with reminders that looked like bank deposits of my new pricing, eventually, that became my reality, and now my phone is pinging all day long with deposit notifications. But I had to first trick myself into believing that it was possible.

Have pretend conversations with clients where you talk about your rates, or share your prices, practice until it feels normal and natural for you. I used to do this a lot while driving in my car. Have full on conversations or pretend to be interviewed on tv or a podcast haha.

Feel into all the value your clients are going to receive in exchange for your service. How will your client benefit from this product or service, what will they feel, what's the outcome they will receive? Once you tap into these feelings, it's impossible to feel misaligned with your pricing.

Journal on all the ways this higher price will add value to your life. Will you be able to spend more time with your family? Will you be able to hire staff? Will you be about to bring on a freelancer #womensupportingwomen? Will you be happier? Thus, a calmer and more mindful mother, partner, or person in general?

Change the prices on your website. You can notify people or not that's your choice. Some people like to make a big deal about it, others don't, what's right for you is right for you.

Use an affirmation like *"People love to pay me, people are excited to pay me, people can't wait to pay me, people love to pay me upfront and in full"*.

Don't back down. It's tempting to still play safe, small, to freak out and let that imposter syndrome run the place, but babe, you're ready for this.

Do it, don't back down, it's the time!

CHAPTER 15

SELLING WITH ALIGNMENT

This section is for the women reading who are in business, self-employed, or in sales. Although relevant for everyone, these principals are universal. The language is geared to an entrepreneur mindset or someone who wants to one day be a part of that group.

When I worked for a large optical company, I used to process tens of thousands of dollars worth of sales every day, I helped little old ladies pick our fun-coloured reading glasses, farmers order safety glasses with their prescription, and kids choosing cool marvel glasses to help with their computer work, etc.

Never once did I question the fact that when I was "selling" all day long, all I thought about was helping people.

The prices were set by the big international company I worked for, the rules were in place, I did the best I could to help every customer who came in the store to the best of my ability. I offered them what I thought would help their situation, and they either took it or left it, or put it on lay by.

I didn't really care much either way, I knew I was doing my job to the best of my ability.

Here is the thing. I didn't take it personally when they said they couldn't afford it this month, I didn't take it personally when they said they would have to talk to their husband, and I didn't take it personally when they did purchase it. I was there to help, advice, and guide, but ultimately, I trusted them to make the right decisions for themselves.

However, when I started my business, it didn't feel like this, I took EVERYTHING personally, because my business was so personal. There was no international company setting prices, I wasn't detached from a potential client's decision, and every part of it, every facet, every "rejection" felt so so so personal.

I kept trying to make sales to book clients and handle objections, but somewhere along the line I needed to tap back into my core values, treat my company like a company and detach a little from every potential client outcome.

It helped so much. Practicing selling with alignment, was truly the game changer for me. When I stopped trying to use every industry tactic for sales calls, objection handling, and BRO marketing and instead, I tapped back into helping people, adding value, and empowering potential clients to make the right decision for them. Don't worry, I'm going to share with you how I did it.

And hopefully this should help you start selling with soul too.

Selling with soul

Think about the last time you checked in on social media for a restaurant or told a friend about a good show on Netflix you are really into, how did you share it? Probably with passion and energy. You probably would not have hesitated to tell them about it or worried about what they might have thought about your recommendation. You just would have shared with love and passion, no emotional attachment to whether they decide to watch the show, go to the restaurant, etc.

Chances are they probably did check out that show, or maybe went and ate at that restaurant, see how easy and fun selling can be? And instead of feeling yucky and eww, if we shift our energy, it can feel really fucking GOOD!

The ONLY reason it hasn't been feeling good or fun so far is because of your energy and attitude around selling. Because you are choosing to believe there are "rules" around selling, and you're likely selling in a way that does NOT align with your soul, personality, and purpose.

What if, and I mean just let's play pretend right now, imagine with me …. what if you just decided right now that it ALL gets to be aligned? What if you decided to see selling as a conversation?

Just passionate, fun, feel-good conversation? Giving people options so they can make the best decision for themselves. DECIDE selling is just GIVING to your soul clients and spreading your passionate message further into the world. When you decide this, you can truly tap into the spiritual and soulful side of selling. It's a lot more fun than sales calls, pressure methods, manipulative marketing, and value stacking pyramids … trust me.

Without aligned selling, you are truly just blocking your highest self from having the true impact you are meant to have.

The universe can't manifest your desires when you are not in alignment with who you truly are and how you truly want to help people. It's time to get out of your own way and let this magic happen in a way that feels REALLY REALLY REALLY good!!!

"Messaging"

Selling from your soul and with alignment comes down to a few key things, so let's break it down.

Messaging and conversion - selling is just messaging, shift your attitude and vocabulary to match this, if the word "selling" makes you feel eww ... switch it to "messaging" instead. It gets to feel as easy as telling your best friend about the new Channing Tatum movie that they just HAVE to see.

Soul Alignment - everything you do in life business and messaging should be aligned to YOU. The same goes for selling, stop buying into the "secret funnel formulae" or "top converting email templates" the more you buy in and try other people's templates, secrets, formulas otherwise known as "RULES" the more you lose YOUR voice. let yourself create, launch, and sell in a way that feels 100% soul-aligned and watch as the clients, impact, and money you desire flow to you.

Belief - you have to 100% believe in your offer, why your soul clients need it. Ask yourself is there anything in your business right now that you are not 100% excited about, that you maybe don't 100% believe in, it is time to let that shit go. If you have stuff you do love, spend some time thinking about how awesome it is, the more excited you are the easier it is to authentically share about it and in turn reach people who need it.

Energy, Excitement, and Passion - are you truly in love

with what you are offering? There has to be a natural urge to share, speak, and yes sell, what you're excited about. Even if you get scared, trust that the natural aligned passion for what you do will nudge you forward and make selling fun.

Is it a HELL YES? - does your offer feel soul- aligned for YOU or was it something you created because "so and so GURU" did one like it. When your higher self is on board and you have created something because your soul prompted you too, your selling, messages, and offers channel from a place of love and flow.Let your higher self lead the way and you will ALWAYS know exactly what to do.

These days In My business I don't do the over hype thing,

The buy now, sell sell sell, pressure, count down, offer offer offer NOW, Guilt, Fear, FOMO … eww no. Just no, it's not needed anymore, it's 2021, it's truly not needed. I am more of a "here is this thing I made, I'm really excited about it, it has my heart in it and I think it would benefit you in x, y, z ways, if you'd like it, it's here for you" type of gal …. Take it or leave it, I'm just here creating awesome shit if you want it.

You don't need convincing.

You don't need to be sold to.

You don't need to be incentivised by sparkly shiny offers and discount codes.

You KNOW ... you know deep inside if this thing is for you or not. And Your client knows it too.

Either way is fine with me.

I strongly believe in this new way because I've seen time and time again how the FOMO hustle brings in all types of wrong clients for me. Something that is purchased from an energy of lack, scarcity, fear, guilt, or FOMO cannot possibly switch gears and help you step into feelings of overflow, abundance, and gratitude. Nope, never works ...

I believe in thinking about it.

I believe in sleeping on it.

I believe in making the soul led decisions.

I believe in truly knowing in your heart that it's the right decision for you, not just jumping on the bandwagon because everyone else is ...

I believe in listening to the FUCK yes in your heart, but also listening to the FUCK no when it pops up. TRUST THAT.

As a business owner,

I believe in creating products and offerings that excite me and light me up more than just market research ideas.

I believe in sharing what I have to offer and telling people about it so that they can decide if it's for them or not.

I believe in creating a business that looks good on paper but that also feels really fucking good in your heart and in your life.

I believe in sharing testimonials and my clients achieving amazing transformations because I'm excited AF for them, and to show what's possible.

And more than anything, I believe in this method, I know deep inside me how powerful it is and It can be for you too if you choose.

CHAPTER 16

BUDGETING LIKE A BADASS!

Do I believe budgets are the be-all and end-all of the money success ...?

NO, I don't * cue controversy

Because I know what it's like to be good at a budget and still broke. To try every single budget available and still have a fucked-up relationship with money (trust me, I've tried them all) ... and I also see people who are super successful, wealthy? and abundant who don't believe in budgets at all.

Should you know how much it costs to run your life ...? Yes!

Should you have a structure in place that helps you hit your short and long-term money goals ...? Yes.

But do you need to count every penny, stack all your money away in paper envelopes, never get take away coffees, haircuts, and any joy out of your life ....?

NO. SOLID NOPE.

Now, when I say I've done it all, I do mean I've done it all. I've done the Dave Ramsey, I've done the barefoot investor, I've made the "smart money", I've done the excel spreadsheets, I've done the yellow legal pad on the fridge. I've ever done "my budget", which was outsourcing all my budget, all my money, all my bills to an agency, and all I had to do was deal with the allowance they gave me every week.

I've done the ......

"No, we can't have that, It's not part of the budget.",

"We can't afford it" when we could,

"You are going to have to wait until next year to get that."

And you know what? None of it helped me tap into the abundance I desired. What did all those budgets do? (it taught me a few skills along the way, don't get me wrong), but it gave me a false sense of control and accomplishment. Like if somehow I could stick to this miraculous budget, every darn thing in my life would be better.

But it did for me what diets used to do .... gave me a restrictive set of rules to follow with the facade of control. And what do we know about restrictive diets ... we know FOR SURE that 95% of them fail. It gave me a benchmark, either I stuck to the budget (which made me a good human), or I blew the budget (flawed human, shame, guilt, anxiety, fear). Restriction, fear, anxiety, shame, guilt, desperation, control .... that's not the type of energy we want around our money. I mean, if the whole point of the law of attraction is to feel good, why would I spend time creating something, like a budget spreadsheet .... that showed me all the things I couldn't have?

Budgets like money aren't good or evil, moral, or sinful .. they are just a tool and a resource. So, once we create neutral emotions around budgeting, it becomes a lot easier.

Energy Math

Half of the budgeting like a badass, is knowing how to do it with the right strategy. The other half of it is about shifting your perspective, aligning your energy with your intention for the budget, etc.

If you're reading this, it hopefully means you're a fan of mine, maybe you've even joined the Elite membership, which also means you've been around my teaching for a Lil bit now... so you're not going to be surprised when I remind you, "energy and intention is everything."

So, let's talk about the energy of budgets, 99% of the time, while a budget is meant to make us feel like we can manage our money better and become healthier, often budgets are deeply steeped in lack, scarcity, and fear. But, if we choose differently and work on our energy, budgets don't have to be about deprivation. They can be about setting conscious intentions about money and energy and choosing in advance what you most desire. Budget = Setting an Intention + Focusing on What you Value = Alignment & Feeling Good.

A healthy budget with long and short term goals will force you to clarify what you most desire in life and help you focus on what is most important to YOU and your family (take note here, NO two budgets should look alike, because no two families will have the same priorities). Once you have clarity over what's important to you and your family, the budget can be used to direct your money and your energy towards what matters most and steer clear of things that you don't value.

When your budget lines up with YOUR values (keyword there being YOUR), you spend more energy on things that make you feel good, which attracts more things that make you feel good. Being honest with myself and my budgets helped teach me so much about myself and what's important to me. For example, we have two areas of our budget that have greatly improved our marriage, entertainment and intimacy ... of which the value is priceless if you ask me, creating a sex toy and date night section in our budget is perfect for us and represents something that is key to our family's functioning (intimacy in our marriage), and supporting women who lead small businesses like Yoni Pleasure Palace is just an added extra bonus. Likewise, we prioritise family holidays and spontaneous bowling trips over private school education, so our "education fund" is split into education and kids' adventure.

Here are my top tips for creating a Budget with the energy of abundance in mind:

- Know your goals. make a list of everything you desire, travel, a lovely home, Hermes handbags, new tits if that's your vibe, food for your family, clean clothes, food for your pets, health insurance, trip to Paris, etc.

- Get clear on what things in this list are the most important to you, IE. What couldn't you live without? If something happened and you had to go into survival mode, what would be the things you absolutely could not go without. For some people, they choose dinner out with family once a week. Some people choose their kids' extracurricular activities. Some people choose to get their nails and lashes done. The point to remember here is there is no right or wrong answer except what is suitable for YOUR family. This isn't about living in scarcity or fear that it all might run out. This is about looking at everything you want and being honest with yourself about it, asking yourself if you want them or if they are one of those "shoulds" that people tell you "should" want or desire.

- Just be honest with yourself, do you value a hot as fuck car over travel? Do you appreciate charitable giving over a Mexican feast with friends laughing till 2 am? Is private school essential to you and your family, or is taking the kids to visit their grandparents in Italy more critical?

  There is no right or wrong answer except what is suitable for YOUR family.

  The best news is that you can have it all. When you start with what you value most, you will attract the rest. Budgets aren't about what you can't have, instead, they are 100 per cent about what you can have. They are about owning your choices.

- Create a Budget that is in alignment with this list of values.

Simple... ok, so it's easier said than done, but you'll get there. download either the sexy selfish calculator or grab a PADTASTIC budget planner.

Remember, this isn't about me giving you a bunch of rules, about what you can spend money on and what you can't. This is about me giving you some guidance and a framework to help you create something that works for YOUR family.

Download the Sexy Selfish Calculator here

https://d1aettbyeyfilo.cloudfront.net/sexyselfish/19873582_1622063902717Sexy_Selfish__Calculator.xlsx

HOW I MANIFESTED MY DREAM HOME.

I knew for a long time that we needed to move into a different home. We bought our old home when we were just 19, we got it for a steal, and it was cheaper than renting. So, we dove in and bought our own home, it was exciting, terrifying, and a lot of responsibility, but it served us well over the years. The mortgage was small, so it allowed us to make some different choices in life.

We brought all 3 kids home to that little 3-bedroom house, and the huge ash tree in the back yard gave us the most delicious shade in summer. Many afternoons were spent on the back lawn, under the shade of the tree, with a glass of wine in hand. I started my spray tanning business from the laundry of that house, and hosted vision board parties from my backyard (champagne included). I met one of my best friends when she came over for a consultation at my dining room table, and I cried in another friend's arms as our babies played in the lounge room after Erik got his Autism diagnosis.

That house we bought, we turned into a home, filled with love and laughter every day.

But baby number 3 seemed to fill up the space in that house, the extra bassinet in our room, the pram shoved in the laundry, the kids growing up and arguing at every point possible, the walls began to close in.

And honestly, I wanted our bedroom to be far away from the kids, they are getting older, and honestly, I was giving less fucks about being quiet in the bedroom. While we are a sex positive family, I didn't want to scare them completely emotionally.

Plus, the whole 1 toilet thing, nothing makes you ready to house hunt faster than the entire family getting gastro and there's only one toilet in the house. NOPE, just NOPE!

But every time we had started house hunting before, we either couldn't even afford to move, never had enough for a deposit, or honestly the houses we could afford just weren't even better than what we already had, so we stayed put for over 10 years.

But as Hudson grew, push came to shove and in the middle of a global pandemic, we decided to start shopping for another house.

While this journey was by no means an easy one and pushed us way out of our comfort zones on multiple occasions, it also proved to be an environment that truly was a pressure cooker for personal growth. Every day as I scrolled the real estate websites, I was forced to remember my affirmations. Every time we put an offer in, I reminded myself to detach from the outcome. Every time we went to an open house, I had to tap into the feelings of it already being ours. Every time we lost an offer, I had to pick myself back up. Every time the tension and stress rippled out and left me snapping at the kids, I had to practice self-care and self-compassion.

It taught me a lot. Mostly the size of your deposit doesn't really make a fucking difference (we had a 6-figure deposit and still had to jump through hoops with so many banks).

But here is the interesting thing. And I guess, the point I want to make.

At the beginning of this journey, I sat down with my husband, and I mapped out what I wanted.

I wanted a house with over 750sqm, I wanted to pay a specific amount, I wanted 4 bedrooms, two baths minimum, I didn't want a house that I would have to spend another 60k renovating, and it had to have a bath and a shed or at least an area where we could put a shed for my husband's work. And yes, before the good reads reviews come in, I am well aware of the privilege of my situation, where I live, and who I am.

Nevertheless, I was looking for a unicorn.

We also didn't want to move the kids' schools, they and we love their school, and for kids with Autism, moving house is already a big change, we didn't want to add into that an entire new school. But this also meant that our options were limited due to location.

A few months into the search, and many disappointments, arsehole real-estate agents and exhausting open houses, I added another thing to that list, which I wanted to buy privately, I was soo sick of real estate agents. I wanted to have a conversation with a real-life person and buy a house from them.

This just turned my already rare unicorn house into a fucking solid gold Pegasus ... everyone told me I was dreaming.

But we held the faith, we visualised, talked about our dream house non-stop, meditated on it and expressed gratitude for the house we had even while looking for our next one.

My mantra became *"it's all working out for us, the perfect house at the perfect time for the perfect price"*

I said it over and over and over again.

But it wasn't just wishing upon a star that got us there, we also looked on real estate sights every day, we contacted all local real estate agents in our area and told them what we were looking for, asking them to contact us if anything came up, we spoke to all our friends and family to let them know we were on the hunt and to keep their eyes open for us, I even went to putting up posters on our local notices board "HOUSE WANTED TO BUY", we went to EVERY open inspection from July – December 2020, made offers on everything, offered above asking price, and went to auction time and time again. I even got to the point of looking at google maps above towns for the land size and location we wanted and popping notes in people's letter boxes asking if they had thought about selling ... I mean I really went all out.

We were so confident that the right house was going to come up, that we packed up our life and put our home on the market. It sold incredibly quickly thanks to our friends at *"one agency property solutions"* and by the 14th of December ... we had to be out. I remember being at brunch with some girl friends, and I had turned my phone off, trying to be present and enjoying my time with them. When the owner of the café, a friend came over and said *"shona your mum is on the phone"*, turns out my husband had tried to call me about 21 times, then resorted to calling my mum, and my mum called all my local coffee shops until she found me (which really tells you all you need to know about my caffeine addiction) …. because our house had sold, cash buyer and we had 3 days to get out. It was intense and mental now that I think back on it. But also, oh so right.

We drove out of our driveway for the last time. As 29-year-olds with 3 kids and a truck load of our life…. Officially homeless and no house for us in the foreseeable future.

I moved with the 3 kids up to my parents' home in the Clare valley, they had some spare rooms and 10 acers for the kids to run wild on during the summer holidays.

My husband's work kept him in the Barossa valley an hour away, so as an almost 30-year-old, he moved back in with his parents for the 6 weeks we were going to be separated.

It was a lot, Hudson's first birthday, my husband's 30th, Christmas, hours and hours of travel between the two homes, being separated from my husband and the kids from their dad was hard. But thanks to face time (phone sex) and some weekends, we were able to catch up and we made it through.

The point, which I'm circling back to now …. Was that we did get our dream home.

When we sold our home we could have never predicted a conversation that would happen a few days later between Aaron and one of his friends who had recently gone through a breakup. They wanted to sell their home and go their separate ways.

A light bulb went off in Aaron's head. Maybe we could buy it?

So, he convinced me to come and have a proper look and we had a conversation with the owners. A quick trip to the conveyancer and an evaluation later, guess what happened?

I bought a house on over 750 sqm, for the exact price I stated earlier, private sale, 4 bedrooms, 2 bathrooms, a bath, and a shed already on it ... the best bit, it was only 2 years old, pretty much brand new.

Buying this house from our friend was so easy, so aligned, so magic, it just happened. There was 0 stress, everyone was happy with the outcome, we handed the Keys over, had a beer and it was ours.

But the clincher is .... never in a million years could I ever had predicted this would be the outcome of all those months of searching for a home. When we first started searching, the owners of this home were planning a wedding .... we could have never predicted that a year later they would sell it to us, in a breakup. And yet through all those hard months I held onto the vision, I didn't know when or why or how or who, but I knew it deep in my bones that it was going to happen, I didn't even let the fear or anxiety that it wouldn't, even enter my body.

"it's all working out for us, the perfect house at the perfect time for the perfect price" I repeated it again and again till I believed it, and then it became my truth.

So, standing in my new home, with the fridge from my vision board, stacking bottles of veuve cliquor in the fridge because you know your girl moved in the most important stuff first, it kind of hit me like a bolt of lightning.

I followed my own manifestation system, the one I teach to hundreds of women … it worked, again, for me.

For years I knew it worked, it gave me Aaron, my career, my cars, my friends, my success, my relationships, my sex life .. everything … but this really was the biggest epic manifestation journey to date.

The one that firmly instilled unshakable, unwavering faith in this process, in my own divine abundant power.

This shit works.

This shit works in ways you could never imagine.

In more ways and often faster than you even thought possible.

It works.

So I've shared this story of buying my home, not to be all *"ohh look at this rich white girl who bought a house"* but to show you, it's the how that always surprises you, it's the faith and trust in the universe having your back that matters, and most of all, it's the hard times that grow us.

I want this book to empower you to trust yourself a little bit more, and hopefully always continue to keep searching for knowledge, leaning into support, keep educating, and keep implementing these teachings.

Because the thing about your relationship with wealth, money, manifestation, and abundance, is not and never will be an overnight thing … it is a lifetime journey of constant evolution.

So, let's wrap it up in a big red bow, silver platter, Cheat sheet style.

My 4-step manifestation system

How to manifest like a badass... So simple, that it almost feels like a trick, but that's the key isn't it, keep it simple. So here is my cheat sheet, the things I come back to again and again, my full proof, rinsed, and repeated system to manifest anything I desire in life.

DECIDE on what you want.

Speak it, write it down, think it, See it.

It really doesn't matter how, as long as you make your DECISION. I know a-lot of people think the "decision" is overrated but there is a reason why every successful person talked about their defining decision .... simply get clear on what you want to attract into your life. CRYSTAL CLEAR. If you can't define it, you can't manifest it. The Universe needs to know the specifics and instructions to deliver on it. YOU ARE IN CHARGE. Specific, sexy goals.

EMBODY the version of yourself that already has it.

This means asking yourself, "If I were to already have this... how would I feel? How would I act? How would I think? What would I say? How would I walk?" This step is all about embodying certainty and realizing that coming from the place of HAVING vs WANTING is where you will shift frequency and become a magnet for what you desire.

SURRENDER

Surrender the "how" and understand that the details of the final reveal will be taken care of for you. YOUR JOB is what & why. The Universe's JOB is the when, how, and who. It's a process of Co-Creation. and your detachment is KEY. Don't be desperate, don't be needy, simply hold the faith, and let there be space for miracles. Do your part, but let the universe do its part too.

STAY ALIGNED Be a soul led babe

You can't expect to receive your desire by skipping past or trying to cheat the Law of Attraction. That law exists because manifestation is a co-creation process. Use your intuition to follow your urges and where you're being pulled to go. Take inspired action, trust your gut, stay consistent and act as if it is already done and dusted ... no doubt, full faith, let your soul lead you and take the next inspired action FORWARD "in the perfect way, at the perfect time"

CHAPTER
18

WHAT NEXT ?

The next step is entirely up to you beautiful. Because only you can know if this work and healing your relationship with money is something you want to dive further into right now, or something you're going to process for a while internally before taking action.

There is no right or wrong, except for what is right for you.

But I believe providing someone with the next steps on their journey is an important part of my work. All of my years teaching this and there is one thing I know for sure ….. this work is a hell of a lot easier when you have a system, support network, and other women alongside you to support you.

This is why I love all my programs,

But the Abundant as F*CK program is a favourite of mine

Because it's so universal. It's for anyone at any stage in life no matter what they have been through or what they have ahead. Industry, age, experience ... it doesn't matter here.

Through this online course, I get to help women all over the world, (in the LIVE SESSIONS) to break free of Money overwhelm, procrastination, guilt, anxiety, and frustration .... and begin relating to their Money in a way that makes us feel good about our desires and inspired to take THE RIGHT action toward them

Because I'm ME, fully unapologetically enthusiastic, we get to do this in a fun, inspiring, healing way together. And that might be my favourite part of all, jumping on every week to the group coaching sessions we do together, getting to know you, your family, your story and working through things together week by week.

The thing is I don't think you are "wrong" for what you have done in the past, like if you have hidden from money, abused money, made hurtful choices with your money.

It's not your fault but moving forward we can create a new reality ... together.

I will not guilt you, blame you, or shame you into change.

I will instead support you, guide you, remind you, and inspire you.

Because you deserve to feel empowered about wealth. you deserve to feel motivated and inspired towards money. You deserve to feel supported and encouraged towards abundance ALWAYS.

The point of all this ....

You get to feel better, you get to have clarity, you get to feel direction, you get to know what your next inspired step is, you get to feel supported, you get to be abundant, you get to have it all NOW.

The intention of this course is to leave you feeling clear, empowered, ready to act, determined and supported in your relationship with money. While also experiencing mental shifts and intentionally manifesting your desires from an abundant growth mindset.

It's time...

It's time to drop the struggle and the confusion around tapping into your inner abundance and knowing what you want so that you have a clear plan and can become an energetic match for your desires.

If you aren't sure what to do, remember this: Your heart's desires are always guiding you.

It's safe to trust yourself.

Say it with me:

I am worthy.

I am deserving.

This is my time.

I am ready to receive.

I am ready to step into my next level of money, love, abundance, and all my other desires.

It's time to heal your history with money, understand the frequency and vibration of money, rework your mindset around money, and set into reality a new blueprint for how you spend, save, earn, receive, release, relate and manifest money in your life.

Click the link below if you feel called to enrol and join me on this powerful journey.

www.sexyselfish.com/abundantaf/

Money Mindset expert and business coach Shona Gates is passionate about helping women worldwide transform their relationships with money.

As a serial entrepreneur and coach, Shona began to notice a reoccurring theme in her development journey and in her clients' mindset work. Money was the block that kept popping up over and over again. Determined to get rid of money guilt for good, Shona spent years transforming her relationship with money, and she vowed that as she learned and mastered this, she would share it with as many women as possible.

Shona Gates has employed different means to reach as many people as possible across the globe. In her online courses, memberships and the new book, she shares her wealth of experience garnered over the years coaching women from all walks of life to embrace the success mindset and get rid of money guilt FOR GOOD.

COACH . AUTHOR . SPEAKER . PODCAST HOST

www.sexyselfish.com @sexy_selfish

Get the Amazon bestselling book GOODBYE MONEY GUILT and totally transform your relationship with money.

The first step in finding financial freedom is to realise that financial freedom has absolutely nothing to do with how much money you have or make. What? Exactly. Financial freedom is something that goes on inside of you. So the first step is to realise that financial freedom is more about our attitudes toward money than about the amount of money.

This book is for women who are curious about mindset work and manifestation but have no idea where to start. The type of woman who deeply desires financial freedom and is ready to learn about creating a positive relationship with money. Shona will teach you the principles of money mindset that will heal and clear your resistance to wealth and show you how to attract more abundance into your life every single day with ease, fun and alignment.

<< Available in paperback, Audiobook or download the EBOOK instantly >>

So, what are you waiting for?

www.sexyselfish.com/goodbyemoneyguilt/

NOTES

Sexy Selfish

DON'T CURRENTLY RECEIVE MY WEEKLY MANIFESTATION
AND ABUNDANCE GOODNESS AND WANT TOO:
SUBSCRIBE HERE:

www.ingramcontent.com/pod-product-compliance
Lightning Source LLC
Chambersburg PA
CBHW050314010526
44107CB00055B/2244